Organizational Processes

Organizational Processes

Francis D. Tuggle
The University of Kansas

AHM Publishing Corporation
Arlington Heights, Illinois 60004

Copyright © 1978

AHM PUBLISHING CORPORATION

All rights reserved

ISBN: 0-88295-455-5

Library of Congress Card Number: 77-86001

PRINTED IN THE UNITED STATES OF AMERICA

Contents

FOREWORD   viii

1. THE CONCEPT OF PROCESS   1
   The Process Approach   2
   Alternative Paradigms   7
   Comparisons of Paradigms   10
   Preview   17

2. GOALS AND GOAL FORMATION   23
   Uses of Goals   25
      Decisional Uses   26
      Descriptive Uses   28
      Exhortative Uses   31
      Analysis of Conflict   34
   Goal Formation and Stabilization   36
   Counterarguments   45
   Discussion   48

3. COALITIONS AND CLIQUES   51
    Theories of Formation Methods   52
       Psychological Theories   53
       Political Science/Economics/
          Bargaining Theories   54
       Organizational Milieu Theories   59
       Process Theories   63

    Areas Affected   67
       Goals and Objectives   67
       Problems Attended to   69
       Reward and Task Systems   70
       Decision-Making Processes   70
       Productivity and Efficiency   71

4. STANDARD OPERATING PROCEDURES   74
    Dimensions of Problematic Situations   77

    SOPs Considered as Decision
       Procedures   82

    SOPs and Organizational Behavior   87

    Designing and Altering SOPs   90

    Examples of SOPs   96

5. MANAGEMENT BY OBJECTIVES   104
    The Method and Philosophy of MBO   106

    The Theory Behind MBO   111

    The Implementation of MBO   113

    Reports from Practice   119

6. ORGANIZATIONAL PROBLEM-SOLVING   125
    Problem Recognition and Formulation   128

    Search Processes   132
       Reactive Search   132
       Circumscribed Search   134
       Opportunistic Search   137
       Idiomatic Search   138

    Normative Search Procedures   142

7. CONTROL AND COORDINATION   150

    Methods of Achieving Control   154
      Reasoning and Logic   154
      Goals   155
      Rules   157
      Power and Authority   159
      Influence   162
      Training and Habit   163
      Work Norm Groups   164

    Relatively Uncontrollable Activities   167

    Methods of Achieving Coordination   170
      Plans, Schedules and Deadlines   171
      Meetings   172
      Feedback and Communication   173
      Decoupling Devices   174

    Overview   175

8. LINE-STAFF RELATIONSHIPS   178

    Development of the Line-Staff
      Concepts   178

    Line and Staff as Issues in
      Organizational Design   179

    Conflict Between Line and Staff   183
      Causes   183
      Effects   187
      Resolution   191

    Staff Groups as Organizational
      Problem-Solving Mechanisms   193

9. ORGANIZATIONAL EFFECTIVENESS   199

    Definitions   201

    Process Framework   209

    Partially Determining Factors   211

    Empirical Studies   216

NAME INDEX   222

SUBJECT INDEX   226

Foreword

The growing awareness of the importance of organizations in our lives has created interest in understanding them. We are interested in individual and interpersonal behavior in organizations. We are aware that organizations influence us and that through our participation we can change organizations. We realize that organizations have subgroups, structures, and task and administrative processes. We understand that organizations are affected by technology, other organizations, and by general social and economic conditions. We also perceive that organizations can be used by their members in order to achieve personal goals.

Given the wide range of problems and issues, there are many theoretical approaches, schools of thought, and very different methods for studying organizational phenomena. This diversity has resulted in a growing, vigorous, and exciting field of study. It has also given rise

to a wide variety of academic courses and research interests.

The books in this series are more than a collection of separate surveys. They have been
integrated to provide a clear picture of the
scope of organizational behavior, to insure
consistency in approach, and to portray co-
herently the relationships existing across sub-
problem areas. Each book cross references the
others, and together they provide an up-to-date
working library for any person seeking to
understand the field of organizational behavior.

To achieve these goals of integration and
completeness, six outstanding scholars and
teachers with experience teaching in business
schools were assembled to write the first six
books in this project. Two are social psychol-
ogists, three are specialists in organizational
behavior, and one is a sociologist. The wide
range of topics was first drawn up and then
divided into six groups. Each of the authors
then worked with the series editor to draw up
a detailed outline for his or her portion of
the whole work. Care was taken to insure that
each author understood how he or she related
to the whole series, that each author had a
theme for each chapter, and that these themes
were consistent within individual books and
across the series as a whole. When the independent writing of each book was completed, the
author and the series editor went over each
manuscript painstakingly to create a solid
part that was consistent with the whole
series. One of the features of this series is
that each book examines its topics in terms of
behavioral processes. Behavior is seen in terms
of complex interrelated sequences of contingent
events.

Each book is written so that it can stand
alone and so that it connects across the others
in the series. Thus, any single book or combination of books can be used in the classroom.

In addition to the coherence of an integrated
series, the integration itself helped to reduce
the length of each book and hence reduce the
direct costs to the student. The author of each
book had the primary responsibility of writing
on his or her assigned topics. But when a topic
from another book was needed, the author could
count on its being adequately covered. Thus,
each author could stick to specific topics and
refer to the other books for more detailed
explanations for other topics. Together these
books provide adequate coverage of the main
topics, a compendium of ideas about organizational behavior, and a source of new ideas and
critical references.

The books in the series were written primarily for beginning M.B.A. students at a respect-
able college or university. Some of these
schools require two semesters or three quarters
of classes in organizational behavior. For
these, we recommend that all six books be used.
Some require a semester of classes. For these
we recommend any three of the books. Those requiring one or two quarters should use two or
four of these books.

Kenneth D. Mackenzie
Lawrence, 1977

1

The Concept of Process

There are many ways in which organizations, and the people behaving in and for them, may be viewed. Some persons see them as rational marketplaces, where such things as power, budgets, problems, time, money, commitments, products, and services are bartered. Others see them as a repository of social forces and abilities that are waiting to be marshaled and channeled so that certain objectives can be optimally attained. Still others envisage them as a system of interconnected elements whose functions must be optimally performed in order for the organization to survive.

In this book, a different perspective of organizations, and the behavior by and within them, is adopted: that of the ongoing processes. It is not yet a common view of organizational phenomena.

The types of organizations for which the theory in this book is addressed cover the whole spectrum—businesses (firms), hospitals, labor unions, educational institutions, political parties, and governments and their many agencies, divisions, and branches. When a model or proposition is limited in its applicability, I will indicate the domain of organizations to which it applies (e.g., firms, for-profit firms, for-profit product-oriented firms, large for-profit product-oriented firms).

The reason for adopting the process paradigm is to try to better capture the dynamics of organizations. They are much more than an organizational chart, a list of functions, or a balance sheet and income statement. Even contingency theories convey an inadequate picture of organizational life. Process theories, like all theories, also simplify, but their simplifications seem less unrealistic.

Parts of this chapter tend to be fairly abstract, as the nature of process models and scientific theories must be discussed. Also, the process paradigm is compared and contrasted to alternative paradigms. Some concepts introduced here will initially seem foreign to you, so I have provided a careful definition. This will facilitate investigations and discussion of process models of organizations and their behavior. Return to the definitions after you have read a couple of chapters of "content" on organizational process. For your convenience, at the end of this chapter there is a preview of the other eight chapters in which the major findings of applying the process paradigm to important organizational phenomena are summarized.

THE PROCESS APPROACH

DEFINITION: A *system* is a collection of interacting and interdependent parts. In particular, organizations are systems, but so are departments and teams within organizations, and so are the individual people who constitute work groups.

DEFINITION: A system may be characterized by describing its state. A *state description* is a list of attribute-value pairs which hold for the system being described at one instant in time.

DEFINITION: An *attribute-value pair* is a dyad: The first part names a property or feature or characteristic of the system under study; the second part gives the particular "score" of the system as measured by the first part.

For example, an individual is a system (his brain interacts with his eyes and hands, for example). We may choose to characterize one such system (person) by use of the following attributes: age, sex, job title, salary, number of years of college, degree of authority, operative Maslovian need, height, sentiments toward person X. Once all attribute-value dyads are listed (e.g., age—35, sex—male, job title—shipping clerk, etc.), one has a state description for that system (person). Since some of the "value" parts of the attribute-value dyads may be different at other points in time, a state description of a system is only known to be valid at one instant in time. It should also be noted that the list of attributes used to generate a state description may be more or less complete (depending upon the purposes to which the state description will be put). For example, if the system under consideration were an organization, and if one were interested in the financial well-being of the system (e.g., its liquidity, debt/equity position, inventory turnover), a list of attributes that does not permit calculation of those financial aspects is incomplete in an essential way.

DEFINITION: The *history* of a system is the sequence of state descriptions of the system over a particular time interval. Similar to state descriptions, the history of a system may be more or less complete. We should not expect the state description of a system to be different from one instant to the next unless some event impinges upon the system. Such events may be of internal origin (e.g., a report is generated within an organization and disseminated, information is assimilated in a new way, a person quits, or a production cycle is completed) or of external origin (e.g., market prices change, information is received about a competitor's future actions, a law suit is started, or an outlet orders more of the product to sell).

DEFINITION: The history of a system is effectively characterized by means of state transition diagrams between each pair of state descriptions. A *state transition diagram* records the initial state, the final state, and the events that transpired between the times of those two state descriptions. However, only those events that influence or affect (or are influenced or affected by) the attributes used in the state descriptions are recorded.

As an abstract example, suppose a system is in state S_1 at time t_1, and in state S_2 at time t_2. Suppose further that events E_1, E_2, E_3, and E_4 have occurred in the time interval (between t_1 and t_2), but only E_1 and E_3 are relevant to the attribute-value dyads used to characterize S_1 and S_2. That is, E_2 and E_4 do not change any of the attribute-value dyads under consideration. Then the state transition diagram for the history of this system from t_1 to t_2 is:

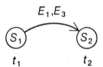

As you can imagine, the state transition diagram for complex systems or for systems with long histories can be unwieldy; abstractly again,

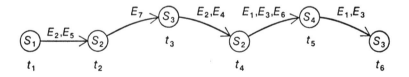

State transition diagrams occur in this book
infrequently; however, they **are** quite prevalent
in Mackenzie(1978). He tends to use the term
task process graph for what we call state transition diagrams; we employ the latter term to be
consistent with the vocabulary of computer
science, the discipline in which the concept
originally arose.

> DEFINITION: A *process model* of a system is a collec-
> tion of rules which account for the history of state
> transitions over the appropriate time interval. The
> rules are propositions about the behavior of the
> system and thus need empirical validation. For ex-
> ample, to account for an observed history of state
> transitions in the system "a pair of people" in which
> the state descriptions focus upon the sentiments of
> each toward the other and a common task, these three
> rules may suffice:
>
> 1. If he shows liking toward me, like him back.
> 2. Else, if he shows indifference to me, exhibit
>   liking or disliking toward him depending upon my
>   sentiments toward the task.
> 3. Else, if he dislikes me, dislike him back.

Observe carefully that (1) many different
sets of rules may be constructed to explain the
same history; and (2) with different state descriptions or different time intervals, different process models may emerge—in particular, the more complete the state descriptions
and the history, the more complete is the resulting process model.

One validates the set of rules by applying
them to the initially observed state, by
positing that the sequence of observed events
in fact occurs in the proper serial relation,
and then by observing whether the generated
state-transition diagram agrees with the observed or recorded history of the system.

A less formal, and less formidable, way of
reviewing a process is as a time-dependent
series of actions for which successive actions

are contingent upon the presence of earlier actions and contemporaneous inputs. A process may be viewed as unfolding in stages or milestones. At the heart of a process is the path followed. The path includes, but is not limited to, the endpoint achieved by the system. Quite naturally, this representation permits the same endpoint to be achieved by multiple paths.

As a simple, but nontrivial and easily comprehended example, consider the sequence of behaviors of *one* of two persons playing a game of ping-pong. The first "swat" of the paddle is easily predicted, but later swats are contingent upon that player's previous swat, his opponent's return swat, and the particular flight and bounce taken by the ball (e.g., if it hits the edge of the table). In short, later behavior depends upon the path of states traversed up to the present (the previous sequence of swats), the previous state (the opponent's last swat), and current input information (the particular flight and bounce of the ball back to the player). It is hard to conceive of another paradigm that could account for this dynamic behavior equally well.

DEFINITION: A system is *process passive* (or *passive*) whenever its behavior, as it moves from state to state across time, is governed wholly by a mapping of stimuli, or inputs, onto responses. Otherwise, the system is *process active* (or *active*). Examples of process passive systems are the free fall of a body in a vacuum, the flight of a ballistic missile, and the effects of certain drugs upon the human nervous system. Examples of active systems are groups engaged in conflict, a person seducing another person, and an organization contesting a government ruling. Other ways of distinguishing between passive and active systems are these: For passive systems, the same set of S-R rules holds true for all states; for active systems, the order in which states are visited partially determines the next behavior. Passive systems receive, or only act upon, one input at each point in time; active systems both receive and attend to

multiple contemporaneous inputs. Passive systems use
the same set of S-R rules for indefinitely long
stretches of time; active systems can and do purpo-
sively change their patterns of behavior.

The response mappings can even be described
in terms of probabilities (as in the case of
the gas laws in physics). Thus, the set of
passive systems includes those with simple
stimulus-response mappings, sequences of stimulus-response mappings where the mapping function is fixed, and probabilistic stimulus-response mappings. Ascribing passive characteristics to all systems regardless of their true
nature is common. Consider how frequently un-
employment is explained by a person's laziness,
and how often consumer demand is said to determine the quantity of goods produced.

ALTERNATIVE PARADIGMS

Before content is supplied to the notion of
process model in the eight remaining chapters
of this book, some appreciation of this approach can be gained by considering and then
comparing alternative paradigms. T. S. Kuhn
(1970) defines *paradigms* as " . . . universally
recognized scientific achievements that for a
time provide model problems and solutions to a
community of practitioners" (p. viii). Paradigms shift over the years, and new ones are
adopted because they can solve the problems
that led the old paradigms to a crisis. Thus,
Newtonian physics gave way to Einsteinian
physics. So a paradigm is the normal, broadly
accepted way of conducting a branch of investigation. The process paradigm will be compared to two alternatives—free will and stimulus-response (S-R).

The systems of interest in this book are
people and their comingling in social entities
called organizations. At the heart of each organizational system are individual people. The
free will paradigm argues that individual

people are not constrained or mechanically determined into making the choices or selections
of behavior that they do. Pushed to its logical conclusion, this paradigm, claims that the
only model for at least some human systems is
a completely idiosyncratic one; that is, the
only way of accounting for the observed transitions is simply to list them all, and there
is no way of predicting the next transition.
In a sense, this approach is ascientific since
it denies the existence of patterns in behavior, patterns which can be concisely explained by rules and laws.

By contrast, the stimulus-response paradigm
asserts that to account for any transition in
a system's history, it suffices to know only
the current state of the system or the input
stimulus. (To generate the next state, one
merely applies the appropriate S-R rule.) This
approach has been quite successful in the
physical sciences and serves as the basis for
many techniques of experimental design, sta-
tistical inference, and methods of modeling
individual and group behavior. It begins with
the belief that there is a finite set of responses and a finite set of stimuli that can
be related by some function. Moreover, the
presence of a stimulus is said to cause the observed or inferred response. It is inherent in
this paradigm that if one knows the response
function, one should be able to predict behavior accurately. Thus, in this paradigm, the
main problems are to identify the types of
stimuli and the range of responses, and to
connect those stimuli and responses by various
mappings of S onto R. This viewpoint is certainly reasonable—if the responding organism
or system can be characterized by such mappings. Skinner (1957) is the leading S-R analyst
and proponent.

One can view these two paradigms as repre-
senting near endpoints on the continuum of
models of systemic behavior, based upon the
amount of information required to predict the
system's next state. Free will necessitates

total information, and even then argues that predictability will be low. Stimulus-response necessitates little information (comparatively speaking).

The uniqueness of the process paradigm can now be seen. While it is not clearly or sharply different from the other two paradigms, it is different in degree. On that same continuum of amount of information necessary for prediction, it occupies roughly a midpoint. The process paradigm argues that the next state of a system is often dependent upon previous states and often upon the time path of states leading up to the current one; that is, systems are capable of learning, and learning depends upon the system's history, the path it has followed. Observe that the process paradigm subsumes the stimulus-response paradigm as a special case, and that the process paradigm approaches the free will paradigm as a limiting case.

Consciously or not, most social scientists have heretofore employed the stimulus-response paradigm in the formulation or the testing of their theories. Any time it is posited that a number of independent variables determine the value of a dependent variable, or regressions are performed, or analysis of variance is calculated, and so on, either the researcher is actively employing the S-R paradigm or he is behaving as though this is the case. Thus, it is not surprising that many social science phenomena lack adequate explanation; the S-R paradigm is occasionally an oversimplification of the system being studied (e.g., see the extant literatures on job satisfaction, motivation and productivity, personality, the determinants of leadership effectiveness). The S-R paradigm assumes a memoryless system, and the S-R paradigm cannot explain how a system will behave when two or more stimuli impinge upon it simultaneously. These and other problems with the S-R paradigm have led to the creation of the process paradigm.

COMPARISONS OF PARADIGMS

In order to be more systematic in the comparison of the three candidate paradigms and to explain further this text's emphasis of the process paradigm to explicate organizational behavior, seven criteria will be described that are often used to evaluate scientific models and theories. In addition, I will consider the procedure by which science explains and predicts events. Then we shall see how the three paradigms stack up against one another. The seven criteria of science are described in roughly decreasing order of importance: validity, prediction, generality, completeness, parsimony, simplicity, elegance.

1. Validity: A theory is *valid* when it fits the facts, when it passes empirical tests and is corroborated. In order for a theory to be empirical (and thus capable of being validated), it must make statements which are capable of being shown wrong; that is, it must be potentially falsifiable (see Popper, 1968). In general, theories are never completely validated—although they may pass empirical tests now, later experiments or results may show deviation. To speak of "validating" a theory is misleading (since that is impossible); the term *corroboration* will be used to mean that the theory has not yet been empirically rejected.

2. Precision: The precision of a theory refers to the level of detail in prediction or explanation (one prefers theories which are relatively precise). Observe that the more precise a theory, the more easily it is falsified. A precise, corroborated theory is very robust and powerful.

3. Generality: The generality of a theory refers to the number of situations it is able to explain or predict. Again, general theories are more readily falsified.

(Observe that some of the criteria of science are in partial conflict with one another—it is *very* difficult to produce theories which are both precise and general. One usually trades one off against the other to produce vague general theories or precise specific theories. To see that precise general theories are possible, consider the science of physics.)

4. Completeness: A theory is complete to the extent that it incorporates all relevant variables, factors, forces, or events into its formulation. An incomplete theory (by definition) cannot be valid (corroborated). Given that one is dealing with a partially valid theory, the expectation is that the more complete it is, the more likely it is to be more widely corroborated.

5. Parsimony: The degree of parsimony refers to the relative number of assumptions, rules, variables, and parameters, necessary to produce a corroborated theory. Of two equally valid theories, science prefers the one that is more parsimonious. (Note that parsimony is in partial conflict with completeness.)

6. Simplicity: In a sense, parsimony "counts" the amount of baggage necessary for a theory to be corroborated, and simplicity measures what use is made of baggage. Suppose it is known that a variable y is determined by another variable x. Then, on the grounds of parsimony, science rejects Theory 1:

Theory 1: $y = F_1(x, z, t, u)$

in favor of the more parsimonious (assumed equally valid) Theory 2:

Theory 2: $y = F_2(x)$

Hempel (1966, p. 41) has a nice example for this situation of simplicity. Consider the three theories to explain the relationship between y and x:

Theory 3: $Y = x^4 - 6x^3 + 11x^2 - 5x + 2$

Theory 4: $y = x^5 - 4x^4 - x^3 + 16x^2 - 11x + 2$

Theory 5: $y = x + 2$

For the observed data:

Y	X
2	0
3	1
4	2
5	3

all three theories are equally valid and equally parsimonious, but Theory 5 is preferred because it is simpler than either Theory 3 or 4 (and, of course, Theory 5 is more precise than Theory 2).

7. Elegance: The elegance of two competing theories is largely subjective, but there is at least one component of elegance that can be factored out for examination—the face validity or plausibility of a theory. Face validity refers to our belief that the theory is valid ("on the face of it"), the degree to which it fits our memory of experiences and agrees with our expectations, hopes, and wishes. Hempel (1966, chap. 4) argues that theories are more readily acceptable the greater their credibility relative to the existing body of knowledge. This is also called plausibility.

Science explains and predicts phenomena using what Hempel (1966, chs. 5 and 6) calls "deductive-nomological" reasoning. Briefly, there is a phenomenon P accounted for ("explained" if P has already occurred, "predicted" if P has not yet occurred, and "postdicted" or "retrodicted" if P has already occurred but you pretend that it has not) by applying a set L of general laws to a set C of specific conditions. If P can be deduced from L conjoined with C, then P has been explained, or predicted, or postdicted, by L. In order for L to be an empirical deductive-nomological theory, there must be two types of laws in L: basic, internal, theoretical principles and bridging principles which connect the basic principles to the conditions. The internal principles

" . . . characterize the basic entities and
processes invoked by the theory and the laws
to which they are assumed to conform" (Hempel,
1966, p. 72). The bridging principles " . . .
indicate how the processes envisaged by the
theory are related to empirical phenomena with
which we are already acquainted, and which the
theory may then explain, predict, or retro-
dict" (Hempel, 1966, pp. 72-73).

The importance of these requirements for
deductive-nomological reasoning can be seen
from investigations into the science of economics. Cyert and March (1963, Appendix A)
call for independent verification of the internal principles of economics; they note that
the hypotheses of economics cannot be strictly
disconfirmed. Clarkson (1963) attacks the status of both the internal and bridging principles of the theories of utility and demand. He
argues that microeconomics is unable to generate " . . . empirically significant predictions
about consumer behavior . . . due to the fact
that the theory of demand is unable to meet
the normal requirements employed in empirical
science" (1963, p. 5). These arguments about
the status of deductive-nomological reasoning
as employed by economics cast doubt on the
status of economics as an empirical science.

Examination of the attributes of theories
and models allows analogous conclusions to be
reached. For example, Gregg and Simon (1967)
show that for a simple concept attainment task,
the process models they construct are more
universal (the term *general* has been used instead of *universal* in this chapter), precise,
and parsimonious than are certain stochastic
theories of the same phenomena; therefore, the
process models are to be preferred.

Now examine these three paradigms—free
will, S-R, and process—in relation to the
seven criteria of science, and then consider
the character of the reasoning they employ.
The matter of validity is an open question and
is likely to be for some time. Scientists,
perforce, reject free will as a paradigm

because of their belief in the existence of regularities in the behavior of all entities, including people and their groupings, in the universe. If there are patterns to behavior, science will codify and explain them. The only way a scientist could accept (empirically) free will would be for all possible models to fail to describe and predict at least one phenomenon. Since it is inconceivable that *all* models will ever be applied, free will as a working hypothesis is rejected. Of course, there are still many phenomena for which existing models do not supply convincing explanations.

The S-R paradigm has been successfully employed to explain and predict a wide range of behaviors, most notably those of the lower organisms. There should be little difficulty with S-R paradigm-based research whenever one is dealing with passive or process passive phenomena. An S-R paradigm is also a good procedure to employ when initially investigating a phenomenon, and it is a good approximation for very short duration responses to simple stimuli. Consequently, S-R paradigms should be relatively more effective for phenomena in physiological psychology (e.g., effects of medication upon the body), psychophysical effects (e.g., music versus noise), and physical systems (e.g., a rock in free fall) than for social psychology, and group and organizational behavior. The longer the period of time between initial stimulus and response, the more active the behaving organism, and the greater the degree of environmental and individual contingency, the greater the shortcomings of the S-R paradigm. As noted earlier, there are a number of human behaviors that have eluded precise description, explanation, and prediction while employing the S-R paradigm. For example, in the field of urban renewal, many people, including social scientists, have the S-R belief that the construction of low-cost housing will have a positive effect on the economic health of a city. This S-R relational statement is based upon simple folk reasoning. Forrester (1969;

1971) indicates that this statement, along
with many others like it, is very likely wrong,
both empirically and theoretically.

Recall that the S-R paradigm is a special
case of the process paradigm. Diagramatically,
a process model might relate S_1 to S_5 as:

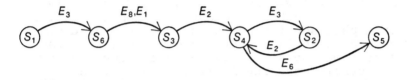

whereas an S-R model might relate S_1 to S_5 as:

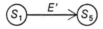

losing or discarding much information. Minimally, the event E' recorded as occurring between S_1 and S_5 disguises the time sequence of
events, which could have been E_3, E_8, E_1, E_2, E_3,
E_2, E_6, or, because of the possibility of
cycling between states S_4 and S_2, which could
have been one of the infinite number of other
possible event sequences. Observe that the process paradigm is more complete than the S-R
paradigm (minimally, because the time path of
behavior is available for use as an additional
explanatory factor). This means the validity of
the process paradigm is bounded below by the
validity of the S-R paradigm. Likewise, the
process paradigm is at least as precise and at
least as general as the S-R paradigm. However,
the process paradigm may be neither as parsimonious nor as simple as the S-R paradigm—but
one employs these criteria only to equally
corroborated theories, and process theories
are at least as well corroborated (meaning that
in general they are better corroborated) as
S-R theories. However, Gregg and Simon (1967)
show that their process models are in fact
more parsimonious than the corresponding S-R
theory. To increase the "intuitive feel" or

plausibility of S-R theories, informal process descriptions of the phenomenon under question are given, and the process by which the stimulus variables affect the response variables is sketched.

Recall that deductive-nomological reasoning consists of a phenomenon P to be explained via a set L of laws applied to a set C of conditions. Altogether too many S-R theories suffer from philosophical defects: C is unstated or is stated in an incomplete or nonoperational manner; L may be similarly unstated, unclear, or untestable; and the logic of application of L to C may be equally fuzzy or questionable. This is not a criticism of the S-R paradigm so much as it is a bad commentary on the abilities of its practitioners and on the efforts used to twist and bend the S-R paradigm to try to apply it to phenomena it cannot explain. But those reasons in combination with another argument to be presented shortly lead unmistakably to the conclusion that the S-R paradigm does *not* permit a cumulative theory of process active systems to be developed. A cumulative theory is one in which findings in one part add to or reinforce findings in another area. Physics has a relatively more cumulative theory underlying it than does history. Most organizational theorizing done to date does not permit accumulation; one person's research and theorizing is largely independent of an irrelevant to the work of other persons in the field.

Consider a system that progresses over time from state S_1 to S_2 to S_3 to . . . to S_n. To explain all these phenomena (the state transitions), the S-R paradigm would typically employ a large number of different sets of laws. L_1 would explain the transition from S_1 to S_2, L_2 would treat S_2 to S_3, L_3 would cover S_3 to S_4, and so on. Maybe some of the sets of laws would be the same. It is rare to find a single set of S-R laws to explain all of the state transitions; it is more common to find multiple sets of laws used and to find that the different sets of laws are at best independent of (and at worst, inconsistent with) one another. When this occurs, and it happens all too frequently with the S-R paradigm, cumulability is blocked. Yet for the same set of state transitions, a single process model will usually suffice. And as more process models are being developed, it is being found that they reinforce, complement, and extend one another. Thus it appears that process models will solve the cumulative problem that has pestered organizational scientists.

The results of this evaluation of these three paradigms are that science reserves free will only as a last resort when no other explanation agrees with the data; that S-R suffices to explain much behavior but fails with some phenomena; and that process techniques may admit an explanation of those phenomena and others, may simultaneously unify many diverse approaches to scientific prediction and explanation, and may permit organizational science to develop cumulatively.

I hold out three beliefs (or hopes) for why it proves desirable to examine organizational behavior from a process perspective: (1) As process theories are, given the evidence, more complete than other perspectives, they are more likely to result in models that are superior in explaining and predicting organizational phenomena. (2) It may be possible to unify and integrate the many diverse existing theories or organizational behavior using a process framework; it may also be possible to develop a cumulative science of organization behavior through the process paradigm. (3) If either point 1 or 2 is accomplished, better understanding and control over organizations will be possible by their managers, by their employees, by those who deal with them, and by an ever more alert public.

PREVIEW

For a person to function capably as a manager, he or she must understand what processes are ongoing in his or her organization, what affects them and what effects they have, and how those processes may be modified to meet new demands. The next eight chapters of this book address some of the more important of those topics that are not treated in the other five books of this series. The coverage is necessarily uneven. Some of the chapters are largely denunciations of the inadequacies of the extant nonprocess models, and these also contain pleas for process formulations to be developed. Other chapters happily trace through process models of phenomena, occasionally praising some particularly insightful discovery. Yet in other chapters, original process models are boldly sketched, leaving for later work the tasks of operationalizing, testing, and refining that crude theorizing. The accumulation of knowledge about organizational phenomena has never occurred smoothly, and this mixed treatment of topics is necessitated by the different levels of understanding about each area that currently exists. The choice of these particular eight subjects rested on three considerations: (1) They are each important in their own right for understanding the functioning of organizations. (2) There is minimal overlap with topics covered in the other five books in the series. (3) The process paradigm is singularly useful in explaining or unifying the phenomena covered by these eight topics.

Chapter 2 discusses goals and how they are formed. Organizations broadcast some goals to their environment to justify and explain their behavior, regardless of whether or not the announced goals bear any logical relation to their behavior. The internal use of goals by organizations is somewhat different. Goals are used internally to assist decision-making and in the attempt to direct, control, evaluate, and motivate behavior, but this is done *without* requiring knowledge of the task processes the goals are aimed at. The futility of this approach is readily apparent, once the organization is examined in process terms. It is naive

to expect task processes to change simply because a new goal or quota or standard has been
announced. Of course, some processes may
change, especially if the change is not a
large one. Some goals can inspire greater efforts, increased sense of purpose, and greater
cohesion, but the fact of the matter is that
if significantly improved performance is
sought, redesign of the task processes is
almost a necessity. If redesign is impossible
or if the current design is already optimal,
then the introduction of new goals is infeasible. We are forced to conclude that the
knowledge of organizational goals alone really
does not convey very much information about
the behavior of an organization, although the
goals may relate something about the nature of
the organization that serves to differentiate
it from others.

Chapter 3 is concerned with coalitions,
cabals, and cliques, informal social (as op-
posed to formal task) groupings that can occur
in all organizations. Presented in this chapter are process models and some nonprocess
models, of greater and lesser degrees of
formality, that purport to explain how these
groupings evolve. Some of the important effects these social groupings have upon formal
organizational behavior are also sketched.

Chapter 4 discusses Standard Operating Procedures, or SOPs. These procedures are used to
react to recurring problems and to make decisions that have become familiar. Most organizations treat most decision situations, at
least initially, as though an SOP will successfully cope with them. So many excellent
process models of SOPs exist that some guidelines for the creation or redesign of SOPs may
be given. The chapter details SOPs for budgeting and other decisions so as to provide concrete examples of SOPs and to demonstrate the
degree of detailed explanation possible in
process models.

In Chapter 5 a relatively new approach to
the area of organizational goals is presented

—Management by Objectives, or MBO. The MBO
approach is to force pairs—made up of a superior and a subordinate—to meet to agree
upon a set of very explicit goals for the subordinate over the next unit of time. At the
end of that unit of time, the subordinate's
progress in regard to those goals is evaluated.
During these meetings, the superior-subordinate
pair may agree to new task processes for the
subordinate. In recounting practical experience with MBO, the results point to small, but
consistent, favorable improvements in performance. MBO is one of the few proven, consistent
techniques for improving organizational effectiveness. While the previous theoretical
justification for MBO has been minimal, it has
proved useful to develop and describe a process
model explaining the reasons for the success of
MBO. Because of the importance of MBO, this
chapter sketches the steps necessary to realize
MBO in an actual, ongoing organization.

Occasionally, problems arise in organizations
that are not amenable to solution via SOPs.
Chapter 6 considers other types of organizational problem-solving. Specifically, a variety
of search mechanisms is examined, each of these
mechanisms being discussed via an informal process model. Certain normative procedures are
considered in some detail, organizational joint
problem-solving being one, both because they
are *normative* process models (a *rare situation* if
there ever was one) and because they are useful for an interesting, complex, and compli-
cated class of problems.

Chapter 7 discusses the twin, intimately related topics of control and coordination. Control is a coordination device, and coordination
is a control mechanism. A number of different
procedures for achieving control and coordination are examined. Again, the relative failure
of these procedures to effect total control
and to ensure complete coordination stems from
ignorance about the underlying task processes.
To reinforce this notion, there is a discussion of a number of relatively uncontrollable

organizational processes. Since even with *complete* knowledge of those organizational processes they prove to be uncontrollable, the conclusion is inescapable that total control and complete coordination are impossible to achieve in practice.

Chapter 8 investigates one important form of intraorganizational conflict, that which occurs between "line" groups and "staff" groups. The cause of a great deal of difficulty in understanding this type of conflict is the lack of a proper definition of what constitutes each of those two types of groups (as you will see, the definition of "staff" groups causes most of the problems). This section shows conflict between them to be inevitable. While some conflict is beneficial for clearing the air and for clarifying issues, that conflict usually has serious negative consequences for the organization in which it occurs. An informal model of the conflict process is sketched so that better management of the conflict may ensue.

Finally, in Chapter 9, we examine the issue of organizational effectiveness. In a sense, this is a capstone chapter, as its theme has been woven in earlier chapters: The organization is a system, the system consists of intertwined processes, and if one wants to improve the organization's performance, the processes themselves will have to be altered. Consequently, the system's resource view of organizational effectiveness is adopted and adapted to fit the process perspective used in this book. This framework allows better understanding of the relationship between efficiency and effectiveness, and permits stronger statements to be offered about factors that help determine the degree of organizational effectiveness.

REFERENCES

Clarkson, G.P.E. *The Theory of Consumer Demand: A Critical Appraisal.* Englewood Cliffs, N.J.: Prentice-Hall, 1963.

Cyert, R. M., and March, J. G. *A Behavioral Theory of the Firm*. Englewood Cliffs, N.J.: Prentice-Hall, 1963.

Forrester, J. W. *Urban Dynamics*. Cambridge, Mass.: MIT Press, 1969.

_____. "Counterintuitive Behavior of Social Systems." *Technology Review* 73, no. 3 (January, 1971): 53–58.

Gregg, L. W., and Simon, H. A. "Process Models and Stochastic Theories of Simple Concept Formation." *Journal of Mathematical Psychology* 4 (1967): 246–276.

Hempel, C. G. *Philosophy of Natural Science*. Englewood Cliffs, N.J.: Prentice-Hall, 1966.

Kuhn, T. S. *The Structure of Scientific Revolution*. 2d. ed. Chicago, Ill.: University of Chicago Press, 1970.

Mackenzie, K. D. *Organizational Structures*. Arlington Heights, Ill.: AHM Publishing Corporation, 1978.

Popper, K. R. *The Logic of Scientific Discovery*. New York: Harper Torchbooks, 1968.

Skinner, B. F. *Verbal Behavior*. New York: Appleton-Century-Crofts, 1957.

2

Goals and
Goal Formation

How can it be possible to understand how, or
why, an organization functions without knowledge of its goals? How can one hope to understand any facet of human behavior, be it individual, organized, or otherwise aggregated,
without reference to "motivation," "purpose,"
"objective," or "target"? In fact, there is a
dispute as to the usefulness of the concept of
organizational goal. Some persons argue that
knowledge of goals permits one to unify, explain, evaluate, and provide direction for behavior. Others argue that goals deceive, not
inform; they feel that knowledge of goals is
irrelevant for understanding the major organizational processes. As we examine the points
that have been raised in the dispute, a middle-
ground position will become clearer: For some
organizational processes, knowledge of goals
is in fact irrelevant, but there are some processes that are largely unfathomable without
reference to organizational goals.

The major reason for the existence of organizational goals is the lack of consensus. If *everybody's* individual preference function were the same, there would be no need for goals to guide, unify, explain, direct, coordinate, and control behavior; there would be no need to do so because no one would disagree or vary from the template. But people *are* different, and so goals *are* necessary.

The traditional treatment of goals embraces the S-R paradigm. Consider the case of an individual person; he is presumed to have a preference function F, and when he is confronted by a situation x, one can predict his behavior to be $Y = F(x)$. (When x is a decision situation, e.g., a list of alternatives, one speaks of predicting his choice y.) Normally, that paradigm underlies the case of organizational uses of goals. In the next section of this chapter, I will indicate the shortcomings of this approach to organizational goals.

If one does not make the bold leap from individual S-R goal paradigm to organizational S-R goal paradigm, the usual approach is to assume that differing individual preferences can be reasonably aggregated into a collective preference. The second section of this chapter discusses a very powerful theory that proves that this aggregation of preferences is in general impossible. Yet organizations do announce goals, and they are cognizant of individual preferences and variance among those preferences, so in some way they are coping with the aggregation problem. The third section of this chapter discusses some empirically observed procedures used to create and stabilize goals.

In the final sections of this chapter, several counterarguments to the goal paradigm are listed that identify processes and conditions for which the concept of goal is not useful.

Let us agree upon a working definition of *organizational goal*, or its synonym, *organizational objective*, as being "a description of a desired future state of the organization or its environment." We choose to leave open, for the time being, the issues of (1) who is doing this desiring, (2) how specific or vague the desires are, (3) what facets of the organization's existence are encompassed by the desires, and (4) what point in time or what span in time that nebulous term *future* refers to. When needed, these open issues will be more carefully specified.

Uses of Goals

Historically, these symbolic constructs called organizational goals have been applied to four categories of purposes: (1) to assist in making decisions, (2) to describe organizational behavior, (3) to exhort the people within an organization to more efficient and more productive behavior, and (4) to analyze the conflicts that occur within an organization, ascribing many if not most of them to conflicts over goals. In the fourth case, there is often a disagreement, sometimes even a power struggle, over who has the authority to set and to change organizational goals and over how broadly that legitimacy may be exercised. Another use is sometimes ascribed to organizational goals: performance appraisal. However, as an organization has multiple, changing, ill-specified goals, using them to evaluate performance is not entirely desirable. The best way currently known to use goals to guide and review performance is given in chapter 5 on Management by Objectives. In chapter 9, means other than "degree of goal attainment" are employed to measure the effectiveness of an organization or its processes.

In the first three categories mentioned above (decision, description, and exhortation), it is commonly accepted that one is referring to the organizational goals of the chief executive of the organization, or at least the few top operating officers of the company. (This is not entirely the case, though, for some disciplines such as economics and business finance do not even admit that executives have goals. Instead, such disciplines assume that the executives hold the goal of maximizing profits or of maximizing owner's net worth.) This is a troublesome position to adhere to vigorously, for at least two reasons. The first is the methodological problem of how one would ever learn what the goals are. Consensus in a group is rare, and individuals are subject to notorious shifts in whims. In practice (e.g., England, 1967), this problem of possible disagreement is ignored; one merely submits questionnaires to the top executives and then pools or averages their responses (e.g., "for your firm, rank order these goals in importance —profit, growth, stability, community welfare, etc."; sometimes this is re-expressed as "allocate a total of 100 points among the following goals to indicate their relative importance").

The second problem, first noted by Simon (1964), is that in a highly interconnected system such as an organization, what are goals to one person serve as constraints to another person, and vice versa. Therefore, to focus attention upon "the" goals of the top person or even the top people in an organization is completely arbitrary. Although arbitrary, it is conventional, and so that is the perspective we shall adopt, ignoring or minimizing the methodological problems as we consider the decisional, descriptive, and exhortative uses of organizational goals.

DECISIONAL USES

In the usual S-R paradigm for decision-making, one needs to know the goals in order to know what choice will result. Further, decision-making is improved (so the argument goes) by thoroughly exploring the goals prior to the choice stage and by laying them out as clearly, completely, operationally, and precisely as possible.

More valid explanations of the role of goals
for decision-making are arising from process
studies of organizational decision-making. For
example, Cohen, March, and Olsen (1972) posit
that organizations are repositories of problems, solutions, and technologies. Sometimes,
an organization searches to find a problem that
may be used with a "good" solution; likewise,
a problem may be sought to be applied to a pet
or favorite technology. Only occasionally do
problems stimulate the choice of a technology
which results in the selection of a solution.
But it is only in this last case that goals
have any relevance for the procedure.

Given what is known about the limited information-processing capacity of people, a more
plausible (and better corroborated) description of decision-making is as follows (see
March and Simon, 1958, especially chs. 6 and
7). When a decision situation is encountered,
a highly subjective, situation-specific model
of it is constructed; for different decision
situations, different models are constructed.
From the model of the situation, action alternatives are developed, an evaluation procedure
is agreed upon, and a set of criteria by which
to judge the alternatives is formulated. Then,
an evaluation procedure applies the criteria
to the alternatives in order to make a choice.
It is important to note that goals (criteria)
result *from* the model of the situation and are
not an independent input into the decision procedure. At a minimum, this admits the possibility of an organization using different, possibly even contradictory, goals (criteria) in
different situations. Even more radical pro-
posals have been advanced; for example, some
such as Braybrooke and Lindblom (1963) argue
that goals are developed *from* the decision
made by an organization (i.e., from its
choices, goals are inferred about what might
be driving the decision-making process), not
that decisions stem from the goals.

About the only role admitted (by the process
study of organizational decision-making) for

broad, global goals is that they in part probably determine (1) which decision situations
will be encountered by the organization, (2)
which decision situations will be actively
sought out by the organization, and (3) which
decision situations, once confronting the organization, will be searched out in more detail to result in a choice and which ones will
be ignored. But the criteria used in a specific, detailed case seem to arise from an interaction of personal preference functions with
the subjective model of the situation.

DESCRIPTIVE USES

Knowledge of organizational goals, it is
claimed, allows one to explain past and current organizational decisions and to successfully predict future organizational choices.
It is easy enough to construct, after the
fact, a goal that will explain past or near-
current behavior; or, given a goal, it is not
difficult to rationalize behavior with it, but
this often becomes a futile task, reeking of
circularism and nominalism ("Why did they hire
more salesmen? They had a goal of expansion.
Why did they appoint a committee to investigate the accident? They have a goal of accident reduction. Why did they close down that
plant? It violated their efficiency goal.").
After the fact, a goal can be found to justify any behavior, and reasoning and rationaliza-
tion can be supplied to bridge the gap between
any given goal and observed behavior.

If conditions are this disenchanting when
it comes to explaining properly current and
past organizational behavior, the use of goals
to predict future organizational behavior must
be similarly shaky. Even when goals are codified in plains, policy statements, and strategy directives, knowledge of them does not permit perfect prediction of the organization's
future behaviors.

These dismal conditions occur because goals
(and plans, policies, and strategies) are at

best statements of intention and preference.
But conditions change—key personnel quit,
fertile markets dry up, new opportunities
arise, and so on. Knowledge of organizational
goals may *assist* one in predicting future organizational choices, but only insofar as they
shed some light on the top decision-maker's
preference function. One should not naively expect that the state described by the goals will
actually be realized.

Similarly, to *explain* the current or past organizational decisions, the crucial point is
to give or infer the minimal set of goals that
is consistent with the decisions to be explained. Analogous problems complicate and con-
found the problem of constructing valid explanations.

Because of the obvious problems in using organizational goals to explain and to predict
organizational decision-making behavior, many
theorists have chosen instead to focus on how
goal accomplishment affects the organization.
That is, rather than erecting theories about
organizations based upon *specific* knowledge of
their *particular* goals, they develop their theories based upon how organizations react to
attainment or nonattainment of their goals,
whatever the details of the goals themselves
may be (profit, cash, sales, inventory, production smoothing, etc.). The best known of
these is aspiration-level theory (see ch. 5 of
Cyert and March, 1963), which has been transported from the psychology of individuals.

The important variables in aspiration-level
theory are: the aspiration level for a particular goal (e.g., one might desire $1,000,000
worth of profits), the current performance or
achievement level (e.g., current profits might
be $500,000), and the rates of change of those
two variables. Finally, there are a small number of rules that describe the interplay between the variables, for example:

• In steady state, the aspiration level always
  exceeds the performance level by a small amount.

- When the performance level rises, the aspiration level increases at an increasing rate.
- When the performance level drops, the aspiration level decreases very slowly.

Then one typically assumes that the rules of aspiration-level theory apply independently to each goal used by the organization under investigation. For further specification, it is not uncommon to find that a small, fixed number of goals have been assumed to capture most of an organization's objectives; for example, Cyert and March suggest that five are sufficient to describe most of the behavior of a firm in an oligopolistic market.

The problem with aspiration-level theory, and others like it, is that it compounds the methodological and philosophical problems of determining the operative goals of an organization. (It is customary to distinguish between the "official" goals of an organization, those found in public relations statements, stockholder reports, and other externally oriented documents and oral messages, from the "operative" goals of an organization, those objectives that are actually used in decision situations—see Perrow, 1961). Although potentially clarifying how an organization reacts to stagnation, success, and failure at achieving a goal, aspiration-level theory does not clarify which goals are selected for an organization, what their relative importance is, how the priorities shift over time, or what use is made of each specific goal. There are several other phenomena that are unexplained: how each layer in the organization comes to develop its own goals (and why the higher layers tend to have official goals while the lower layers tend to have operative ones), how goal elaboration occurs in which high-level official goals constrain the development of lower-level operational ones, how goals are revised through interaction with the organization's environment (but see Thompson, 1967), and how goal displacement

occurs in which a goal that has been attained
once and for all is dropped from consideration and a new goal instituted in its place.

EXHORTATIVE USES

Consider for a moment the top manager of an
organizational unit (including the chief executive of the entire organization). It is argued that it is to his benefit to have a set
of goals for his unit, to understand and accept them, and occasionally to articulate and
explain them to his subordinate personnel. By
so doing, a number of virtues can be obtained
—direction is readily supplied for the efforts of the subordinates, their activities
can be more easily coordinated (see also chapter 6 of this book), unification of their behaviors can be attained, their motivation can
be increased so more efficient and effective
performances result; and the evaluation of
personnel and the missions and programs in
which they are engaged is facilitated. In
short, knowledge of organizational goals can
be put to exhortative purposes.

Before examining these claimed exhortative
virtues more carefully (direction, coordination, unification, motivation, and evaluation),
let us fully cede the indisputable benefits
that organizational goals can supply for each
individual member of an organization: a sense
of identity, a personal purpose, a solution to
his anomie problem, and an answer to the exis-
tential question of "Why am I?" Each of us
achieves these benefits by accepting and identifying with a set of goals for some (possibly
several) organization(s).

These real benefits notwithstanding, the
other exhortative values claimed may be more
apparent than real for several reasons. First,
it is rare for the top manager of a unit to
verbalize all or even most of the goals he expects and desires his subordinates to adhere
to, and because of the well-known frailty of
human memory, it is even rarer for his

subordinates to remember all he said or wrote. Thus each member of every organizational unit has at best a partial, shifting picture of his unit's goals, hardly the sort of thing re- quired for coordinated, unified efforts.

Second, the set of goals used in a unit must be paralleled, in order to be effective, by the reward system. If not, the people will quickly learn they are being exhorted to do one thing and rewarded to do another; in most cases, people will usually adhere to the re- ward system. But even mirroring the set of goals with the reward system is very hard to do, harder even than evaluating personnel and program performance against the operative set of goals (performance evaluation is obviously a necessary precursor for the reward system). The reasons are more thoroughly discussed in chapter 5 of this book, but to sketch the problems: Most organizational goals are not stated precisely enough to permit fair judg- ments to be made; most goals are broadly ap- plied so that determination of differential individual contribution is not easily made; and most organizational goals are given to, not negotiated with, the subordinates they affect. Therefore, in practice, the set of goals of a unit usually bears only a tenuous relation to the reward system in effect, and this is not functional for motivating, direct- ing, or evaluating the behavior of personnel or programs.

Third, it is altogether too frequent to find that the members of different organizational units fiercely hold goals, especially goals that serve to distinguish and differentiate each unit from all of the others. This phenom- enon has been called *subunit identification* (see March and Simon, 1958, ch. 3), and it results in suboptimization. That is, each unit in the organizational system may optimally achieve its own goals, but the effect upon the total system is to degrade total system performance. Suboptimization occurs because no one knows how to factor optimally the global, overall system-wide goals into the correct set of sub-goals for each subunit. Instead, the goals used by each unit in an organization are only a crude surrogate or rough approximation to what the subgoals *should* be. The upshot of this is that one should occasionally, for the good of the entire system, be willing to have the performance record of his own subunit look bad. (For example, inventory control clerks should be willing to allow their stock to be completely depleted occasionally. It makes them and their unit look poor, but the entire system enjoys larger revenues.) And of course, the greater the identification with individual units; the less likely this system-wide perspective will be employed in the subunits, and the more likely is suboptimization. Yet subunit identification is more likely to occur the more the manager of a particular unit emphasizes that unit's goals.

Fourth, the goals that are exhorted are usually given in the absence of statements about the underlying task process. It is as if the superior believes that by setting more difficult goals, quotas, or standards, the subordinates will respond by "discovering more efficient ways to do the job on their own." Because the goals are usually set in isolation from the task processes, what usually results are problems with human relations (interpersonal conflict, aggression, etc.), grievances, strikes, failure to meet the goals, and so on. Exhortative goals *may* change the *degree* of vigor put into task processes (the subordinates may in fact "work harder"), but they almost never change the *type* of task process used (their hard work may be no more effective or efficient). If a change in task process is desired, exhorting greater efficiency and effectiveness will almost never accomplish it.

The conclusion to be drawn is that one must use organizational goals in an exhortative fashion carefully. Probably the best way found to date is treated in chapter 5.

ANALYSIS OF CONFLICT

The last purpose to which knowledge of organizational goals is usually applied is the analysis of several classes of intraorganizational conflict. Three such classes are (1) the individual versus the organization, (2) informal interpersonal or interunit conflict, and (3) formal interpersonal or interunit conflict.

Several contemporary writers (e.g., Argyris, 1964) trace many human problems to a lack of congruence between organizational goals and personal goals. This difference in goal sets, it is claimed, leads directly to personal problems such as frustration, apathy, alienation, low productivity, dissatisfaction, resentment, and the onset of neuroses. These problems also stem from the differences in clarity of goals set: The individual is cognizant of a small, clear, relatively precise set of goals (his own), yet he senses that the organization's goals are less clearly defined, less tangible, and less stable than his own. Individual people tend to get caught up with day-to-day existence and survival. As a consequence, their goals tend to have a short-range focus and tend to be relatively more operational. An individual is thus likely to have a greater proportion of operational goals than organizations do.

The second class of intraorganizational conflict, informal interpersonal and interunit, largely stems from what is called a lack of value sharing (see Seiler, 1963). When two individuals, or units, discover a lack of value sharing, conflict typically ensues; for example, a power struggle to establish the superiority of one position over the other, or to destroy the credibility of one side, or to have one party's personal goals legitimatized as the formal goals. The usual procedure is to learn what the operative goals are when interpersonal or interunit conflict is discovered. From this knowledge, one can attempt to resolve the conflict intelligently (that such conflicts deserve resolution is taken as being self-evident—they detract from the efficient functioning of the organization). Perhaps there is some common ground, or perhaps conciliation will succeed, or maybe one should introduce a set of superordinate goals, or perhaps the only way to eliminate the conflict is to sequester all relevant parties in a T-group until they emerge with an understanding of, and tolerance for, each other's position. (Superordinate goals are broad, all encompassing, unifying goals that cause "minor" differences to be ignored. A typical superordinate goal is to find some real enemy in common with each of two parties in dispute. The presumption is that the superordinate goal will cause the lesser value differences to be overlooked (see Sherif, 1956). T-groups, or Training-groups, are nondirective assemblages of people who learn about interpersonal processes, about the effects of one person upon another and upon the group, and about the effects of the group upon himself. See Bennis, et al., 1968.)

The third class of intraorganizational conflict, formal interpersonal and interunit, arises in part from substantive disagreements over what the nature of a unit's formal, operative goals ought to be. As discussed by March and Simon (1958, ch. 5), these conflicts are manifested in four ways, the particular way exhibited depending upon the operationality of the goals in question and the degree to which the two conflicting parties are interdependent. (A goal is operational to the extent that its degree of achievement can be objectively ascertained. Clearly, operationality is measured on a continuum. The goal of "reducing inventory by 5% is reasonably operational; the goal of "maximizing the public welfare" is relatively nonoperational.)

Analytic processes are used to resolve conflicts when there are shared operational goals. It suffices for one party to be shown "right" and the other party "wrong" to

terminate the disagreement. *Persuasion* can be
used when the goals are still toward the operational end of the continuum, though not fixed.
Bargaining may be used when the goals are nonoperational and there is a continuing sense of
close interdependency between the parties in
conflict, but *politics* must be used when the
goals are nonoperational and the sense of
close interdependency is lacking.

For all three classes of goal conflict,
knowledge of the relevant organizational goals
permits one to diagnose the conflict and suggests steps that may rectify or ameliorate it.
However, as most serious students of intraorganizational goal conflict are quick to admit,
efforts to resolve conflicts over goals probably enjoy the lowest success rate of work at
conflict minimization. The situation is analogous to the one of trying to convert the beliefs of a religious zealot: Success is not
likely. So again, unfortunately, knowledge of
organizational goals is not as fruitful as
one might either expect or desire.

GOAL FORMATION AND STABILIZATION

There is a remarkable result discovered by
Kenneth Arrow (see Luce and Raiffa, 1957, ch.
14) that groups, and, similarly, organizations,
are in general unable to aggregate individual
preferences into a group preference in a
"reasonable" way. To sketch the Arrow Impossibility Theorem, he posits five "reasonable"
conditions that an aggregation procedure
should satisfy and then proves that there are
no procedures that simultaneously meet all
five conditions. To overview the five conditions:

1. There are at least two people in the group,
   and there are at least three alternatives
   from which to choose,

2. The results of the aggregation procedure
   are not altered by changes in the rank order
   of lesser preferred alternatives.
3. The rank order of a set of alternatives is
   not changed by adding new ones (though the
   new ones may be more or less preferred than
   the old ones) or by deleting some (i.e.,
   of those remaining, the rank order remains
   the same).
4. No aggregation procedure may be forced upon
   the group.
5. No one person may dictate an aggregation
   procedure to the group.

As an example, suppose that there are three
people, A, B, and C; that there are three
alternatives x, y, z; and that:
   A prefers x to y to z
   B prefers y to z to x
   C prefers z to x to y
Then, two out of three people
   prefer x to y (A and C)
   prefer y to z (A and B)
   prefer z to x (B and C)
What should the group choice be? There is no
"reasonable" procedure to answer that question.
   The implications from the Arrow Impossibility
Theorem are that it is in general impossible to
aggregate "reasonably" individual preferences
into a group preference. Stated differently,
although individuals have goals, groups and
organizations should be unable to have them.
But, empirically, organizations *do* have goals.
This section addresses the means people use to
muddle through the dilemma to avoid facing the
difficulties posed by the Arrow Impossibility
Theorem.
   There are four major empirically based types
of theories that deal with the origins of an
organization's goals: Those dictated by the essential task confronting the organization,
those arising from the personal preferences
of the key people in dominant positions in the

organization, those evolving as the organization experiences a greater history of interacting with its environment, and those emerging
as the side effects and conditions necessary
for the organization to solve the problems with
which it is confronted. (As usual, the truth
is probably some subtle blend of all of these
theories and possibly others.) After discussing these four goal-formation theories, we
shall consider a variety of goal-stabilization
devices employed by organizations, that is,
procedures they use to ensure a degree of
continuity of goals over time.

Charles Perrow (1961), in his studies of
hospitals and other institutions, found that
their goals were predominantly shaped by the
essential tasks they were facing. Perrow described four types of tasks: (1) the formation
and maintenance of sufficient capital (e.g.,
the mining industries), (2) the recruitment,
training, and marshaling of labor (e.g., small
appliance assembly industries), (3) the codification and adherence to a system of rules
(e.g., civil service agencies), and (4) the
coordination and application of skilled professional workers to problems (e.g., consultant firms). There is also a fifth category
which is "some combination of the other four."
With Perrow's theory as a starting point, one
can easily envision two phenomena. First is
that of the maturing organization encountering
each of those four tasks as the essential one
at different stages in its growth and development, and continuing, cyclically, to face them
again over time. The second phenomenon easily
conceived is that of a large bureaucracy whose
subunits are independently and simultaneously
addressing each of those tasks: a treasury
division battling the capital task, a personnel division wrestling with the labor task,
line management fighting the rule task, and an
R & D department confronting the skills task.

One possible criticism of Perrow's theory is
entirely empirical in nature: He has not found
the exhaustive and exclusive list of essential

tasks which organizations face. Another criticism is that too many real organizations are only correctly described by his miscellaneous category, that their essential tasks shift too rapidly to allow one single, stable goal to coalesce. That too is an empirical question, open to further corroboration attempts. However, the crucial theoretical question is whether the tasks cause the goals to be formed and then the management team developed to work toward that goal, or whether the process works in the opposite direction: A management team is formed and they discover that they are effective at one type of goal; therefore, a task consistent with that goal is selected. Whatever the true nature of the cause-event chain, it is largely indisputable that there is a correlation between the essential task facing an organization and the primary goal formation of that organization.

Another theory of organizational goal formation is stated by Cyert and March (1963, ch. 2). Their theory is predicated upon the proposition that "individuals have goals; collectives of individuals do not." In their view, what is typically referred to as the set of organizational goals is but a reflection of the desires of the key people shaping the destiny of the organization. They refer to the collection of key people running the organization as its "dominant coalition," to correctly suggest that they are a loose, shifting band of people that currently wield sufficient power collectively to see their wishes translated into organizational action. Each person in the dominant coalition provides resources that can be applied and a set of demands and problems that must be attended to. The "glue" that holds the dominant coalition together is the willingness to pool and marshal resources to meet constituents' demands and to solve their problems. Since not everyone's demands and problems can be attended to simultaneously, "side payments" are effected. A *side payment* is an indirect inducement one person or clique offers another.

It may be a promise of future assistance, it
may be a nonmonetary reward, but whatever its
form, the function of a side payment is to
secure continued participation in the coalition. (For more information on cliques and coalitions, see chapter 3).

Cyert and March argue that the operative
goals of an organization arise from the characteristics of the persons in the dominant coalition, specifically, from the set of demands
made upon the organization's resources, from
the set of problems that need attention, from
the relative urgencies of demands and problems
(in part determined by the relative power of
each person in the dominant coalition), and
from the set of side payments necessary to
keep the coalition viable. Note that the Cyert
and March theory of organizational goals predicts that goals will shift as demands, problems, resources brought, and side payments
shift, whether that is due to the satisfaction
of old ones, the origination of new ones, or
just a shift in membership, with a commensurate
change in demands, problems, resources, and
side payments.

For example, imagine a two-product firm that
is functionally organized; suppose that, for
whatever reason, the dominant coalition consists of the president, the two marketing vice-
presidents, one vice-president for production,
and the head of the research and development
group. The goals engendered by that firm are
likely to be quite different from a second,
similar firm whose dominant coalition consists
of the two production vice-presidents, the head
of the engineering group, and the president.
The differences in goals in these two hypothetical firms are due to differences: (1) in resources commanded (advertising, distribution,
selling, and innovating capabilities in the
first case; manufacturing and inventorying
capabilities in the second); (2) in the problems that are considered worth attending to
(figuring out what customers want and need now
and in the future, in the first case; figuring

out how to make operations more efficient, in
the second; (3) in the demands that are made
upon the organization (high quality products
and production flexibility, in the first case;
product standardization and cost minimization;
in the second); and (4) in the types of side
payments necessary to keep the coalition bonded
together (in the first case, budgetary commitments for R & D and marketing research are
traded for promises to continue to develop new
products with marketable features; in the second case, capital expenditures for machinery
are agreed upon in trade for increased autonomy
for maintenance personnel, increased overtime
utilization, and increased authority for the
purchase of raw materials).

A third theory of organization goal formation
is that goals are formulated on the basis of
the organization's experience and history with
its environment. As the organization interacts
with its environment, it may learn that it is
good at some activities (e.g., building and
selling cars), not so good at other activities
(e.g., producing and marketing paint), and just
terrible at yet other activities (e.g., whole-
saling food products). From its successes and
failures, an organization expands, contracts,
or keeps constant its activities. (Thus, as
the Ford Motor Company experienced success
with its Mustang, it developed goals to produce more of them and to market them more intensely. Compare those goals with Ford's goals
for its Edsel and its Mercury.) This theory
also permits shifts in organizational goals because of changes in demand patterns, competition, the general economic condition, and random fluctuations in all of them.

A fourth perspective or organizational goal
formation is that goals arise as a result of
the group problem-solving that goes on in organizations. This theory posits that (1) as
problem-solving goes on, choices must be made
and goal statements are crystallized from the
stream of choices that ensue, and (2) as the
groups attempt to solve the problems, it

becomes apparent where the central difficulty lies, and goals are constructed to remove or reduce those troublesome features. Similar to the Cyert and March theory, the problem-solving occurs in groups and coalitions, but in contrast to their theory, *all* groups in the organization, not just the dominant coalition, can have an impact upon the formation of organizational goals, and the problems are not so much identified with particular individuals as they are seen as arising in the course of the organization transacting its affairs.

Whatever the manner in which an organization's goals are formed, be it from the required tasks, the characteristics of the dominant members, the history of the organization's ups and downs, the stream of problems it faces, or some other as yet unstated process, it is certainly the case that those goals, once created and agreed to, are elaborated upon, institutionalized, and stabilized through a variety of mechanisms. Those people responsible for a goal going into effect do not want to see their hard work prove fruitless in a week or a month or so; they are motivated to ensure that the goal enjoys some permanence. Four of the chief elaboration and stabilization devices are (1) budgets and contracts, (2) plans, policies, and strategies, (3) organizational design, and (4) shared commitment.

For an organization to take action, scarce resources (e.g., dollars) must be consumed. Before they are used, resources must be authorized to be expended—the two major forms of authorization are budgets and contracts. When an organization creates an action goal (or modifies an old action goal) which requires a change in resource level, that nonoperational goal is made more operational (i.e., is elaborated) by its budget or contract level. For a company president to argue for "more vigorous marketing research" is one thing; for the budget of the marketing research department to be increased by X dollars (or for a contract

with the WYZ marketing research firm to be let
for X dollars is quite another. The original
goal is nonoperational; the budget or contract
for X dollars is more operational (it estab-
lishes an upper limit on what can be accomplished). Besides elaborating upon and insti-
tutionalizing the original goal, budgets and
contracts also introduce a degree of stability
to it—the goal will remain in force as long
as there remain budget or contract resources to
be consumed. Of course, the longer the term of
the budget or contract (e.g., one year, three
years, five years, ten years, . . .), **the**
greater the stability.

A second way that goals are elaborated and
stabilized is through plans, policies, and
strategies. A *plan* is a detailed, future-ori-
ented statement of activities the organization
anticipates being engaged in; the activities
may be sequential (in six months we'll do A,
then three months later we'll do B), and they
may be contingent (if one year from now A_1 is
the case, then we'll do B_1; else if A_2 is the
case, we'll do B_2). (*Planning* is the procedure
of developing that scheme of action.) A *policy*
is an inward-directed rule, sometimes stated
abstractly, to guide the behavior of the members of the organization (e.g., "henceforth,
there will be no smoking in the lunchroom," or,
"after January 1, all workers are to remain at
their job stations until at least 4:58 PM").
Sometimes policies are implementations of
plans. A *strategy* is an abstract, future-ori-
ented, outward-directed statement of where the
organization would like to be with respect to
its market, competitors, industry, and environment in general. The details of how the organization expects to achieve that position are
specified through plans.

By translating a goal into a plan, policy, or
strategy, one necessarily supplies a more detailed picture of the goal (thus elaborating
upon it) and, at the same time, communicates a
sense of continuity to the goal, at least over
the relevant life span of the plan, policy,

or strategy (thus adding stability to the goal).

The very design (or redesign) of an organization is a third procedure for elaborating upon and stabilizing organizational goals. Organizational design encompasses a number of issues (for greater detail, see both Mackenzie, 1978, and Pfeffer, 1978), such as the authority structure, the communication structure, the division of labor, and the work flow. Many organizational goals can be, and are, translated into organizational design considerations. For example, a desire for more rapid decision-making may involve shifting the locus of authority; as the organization desires new missions to be accomplished, new subunits may be created; a drive for greater efficiency may lead to a reduction in the number of personnel, etc. To translate a goal into a changed organizational design is clearly to elaborate upon the goal. Furthermore, since the design of an organization in practice is not easily, readily, or rapidly changed (see the chapter on organizational change in Pfeffer, 1978), to change the design is to stabilize the organization's goal.

The fourth technique for elaboration upon and stabilization of an organizational goal is through shared commitment. Basically, this consists of getting universal agreement throughout the organization to this goal and to the more operational subgoals derived for the relevant units and persons throughout the organization. In the extreme, this process of shared commitment becomes management by objectives (see chapter 5 of this book). Clearly, this process elaborates upon the goal by virtue of the more specific subgoals created and implemented, and this process stabilizes the original goal owing to (1) the large number of people who now adhere to it, and (2) the difficulty one would have in changing the beliefs about the desirability of the goal, beliefs now held throughout the organization (recall ch. 7

on Balance, Congruity, Dissonance, in Jabes, 1978).

COUNTERARGUMENTS

There are a number of counterarguments against the utility of studying organizational goals regardless of whether that study is based upon the S-R or process paradigm. Three will be presented here: One that argues "misdirection," a second that argues "irrelevant," and a third that argues "invalid."

Georgiou (1973) criticizes the entire field of study (and of potential uses) of organizational goals as being misaimed. Akin to Cyert and March, he feels that the very concept is a fiction, an inconvenient one. He argues that individual people have interests, but this legal entity called an organization cannot have goals. He proposes that the science of organizations would progress more rapidly were it to study the personal interests of individuals and how they form, evolve, and interact, rather than impotently studying the so-called goals of organizations. He goes on to show how goal-like conceptualization has permeated our thinking, to the point where it is paradigmatic. He would have the field follow his proposed counter-paradigm.

A second objection is that the concept of organizational goal is simply not needed to understand the crucial organizational decision-making process. For example, both Braybrooke and Lindblom (1963) and Cyert and March (1963) posit, and to a large extent verify, models of organizational decision-making that do not make reference to the concept of organizational goal. Instead, their models are of "muddling through," where the chief mode of decision-making is through the "standard operating procedure" (see chapters 4 and 6 of this book). Indeed, Braybrooke and Lindblom (1963, p. 93) go so far as to argue that organizational

goals, rather than *determining* choices, are
developed and inferred from the decisions that
are made.

For example, in the Braybrooke and Lindblom
model of organizational decision, the first
stage in the process is typically *not* to clarify goals and values, and later stages are
typically *not* to select an action alternative
because it can be shown to be the most appropriate means to the desired ends. Instead,
it is recognized that there is widespread
disagreement over goals and values and that
even individuals may be unable to rank order
their personal preferences reliably. This
buzzing confusion is resolved by letting the
goals emanate, in part, from the available
alternatives by evaluating what they offer at
the margin (thus, this becomes decision-making
by incrementalism). If there are two action
alternatives A and B and both offer the same
degree of attainment of objective x, but A
offers more of y than B does and B offers more
of z than A does, then the choice between A
and B rests upon the marginal value of y versus the marginal value of z. Overall organizational goals are *not* being utilized in this
process.

Also, the organization is able to make a
decision without having to agree upon a set
of criteria and without having to show that
the chosen alternative optimally attains those
criteria by simply garnering enough support
for one alternative. A decision is "good" if
sufficient people agree to it, without having
to specify for what ends it is good. Many people or factions may support the same alternative because they see it as beneficial for
their own individual purposes, without having
to reach a global group consensus on objectives (this is another route around the Arrow
Impossibility Theorem).

Finally, decisions are not made to attempt
big jumps toward ultimate goals. Rarely do
organizations move toward some end; more
frequently, they move away from problems and

uncertainty (see Thompson, 1967). Instead, successive limited comparisons (i.e., muddling through) occur—"successive" to suggest a series of changes introduced continuously over time (to try to take readings on the nature of the environmental uncertainty), "limited" to suggest that each change is small on a relative basis (so if wrong, corrections can be made easily), and "comparisons" to suggest the incrementalism in the decision-making (incrementalism so a decision can actually be reached).

The picture of the organization that is painted by this point of view shows the organization wandering through its existence, making minor, midcourse adjustments as conditions dictate. This in contrast to a goal-driven organization which introduces major changes so as to keep its central purpose in clear focus.

The third class of complaints against the utility of the concept of organizational goal argues that empirical study and observation of top-level managers does not find them dealing with goals, except in terms of public relations. Mintzberg's (1973) studies lead one to characterize the behavior of upper-echelon managers as being "situational reaction." That is, those managers reacted to situations (crises, problems, routinely scheduled meetings, telephone calls, chance encounters, etc.) as they arose. What did *not* characterize the managers was deliberation, careful planning, reflection, and the creation and use of goals. When decision alternatives were presented, a choice was hurriedly made; there was no recourse to goals. In some instances, the stream of choices made were inconsistent with one another; in at least one case (see Mintzberg, 1973, pp. 74-75) the inconsistency in choices was deliberate—the manager did not wish his subordinates to be capable of predicting his behavior! There is definitely no use being made of formal organizational goals in these cases.

DISCUSSION

What is to be made of organizational goals? As you have seen, there are several very plausible theories of organizational goal formation and elaboration for which there is some empirical support, but there are also several very telling counterarguments. Are organizational goals useful for understanding organizational processes?

In one very real sense, the existence of this dilemma is due to the relative immaturity of the field of organizational science; enough is not yet known about these things called organizations. The field is ripe for good research and insightful researchers.

In another sense, *everybody* is right in this debate; it is a matter of the phenomenon of interest (organizations and their behavior) being so complex that in order to grapple with it successfully, one simplifies and, knowingly or unconsciously, focuses upon but a part of the phenomenon. So Georgiou is of course right when he says an organization is nothing more than a collection of individuals with personal interests; Braybrooke, Lindblom, Cyert, and March are all correct when they note that for many decision cases no reference to goals is needed; and Mintzberg is right when he finds goals rarely being used by managers in actual studies of workaday behavior.

However, as noted in this chapter, goals are created (or at a minimum, inferred from upper managerial behavior) and used for a variety of purposes for which nothing else seemingly will suffice—good public relations, exhorting subunits to greater levels of performance (but not different *types* of performance), supplying identification and existence for individual people, analyzing several classes of conflict that occur, etc. Reference may be made to formal organizational goals infrequently, and loosely (so inconsistencies may appear), and it may be possible to study many organizational phenomena without invoking the concept of

"goal" and by only referring to individual interests, but the reality of organizational
goals to the people actually serving in organizations cannot be denied.

REFERENCES

Argyris, C. *Integrating the Individual and the Organization*. New York: Wiley, 1964.

Bennis, W. G., Schein, E. H.,Steele, F. I., and Berlew,
D. E. *Interpersonal Dynamics*. Homewood, Ill.: Dorsey,
1968.

Braybrooke, D., and Lindblom, C. E. *A Strategy of
Decision*. New York: Free Press, 1963.

Cohen, M. D., March, J. G., and Olsen, J. P. "A Garbage
Can Model of Organizational Choice." *Administrative
Science Quarterly* 17, no. 1 (March 1972): 1-25.

Cyert, R. M., and March, J. G. *A Behavioral Theory of
the Firm*. Englewood Cliffs, N.J.: Prentice-Hall, 1963.

England, G. W. "Organizational Goals and Expected Behavior of American Managers." *Academy of Management
Journal* 10, no. 2 (June 1967): 107-117.

Georgiou, P. "The Goal Paradigm and Notes Toward a
Counter-Paradigm." *Administrative Science Quarterly*
18, no. 3 (September 1973): 291-310.

Jabes, J. *Individual Processes in Organizational Behavior*. Arlington Heights, Ill.: AHM Publishing
Corporation, 1978.

Luce, R. D., and Raiffa, H. *Games and Decisions*.
New York: Wiley, 1957.

Mackenzie, K. D. *Organizational Structures*. Arlington
Heights, Ill.: AHM Publishing Corporation, 1978.

March, J. G., and Simon, H. A. *Organizations*. New York:
Wiley, 1958.

Mintzberg, H. *The Nature of Managerial Work*. New York:
Harper and Row, 1973.

Perrow, C. "The Analysis of Goals in Complex Organizations." *American Sociological Review* 26 (1961): 854-865.

Pfeffer, J. *Organizational Design.* Arlington Heights, Ill.: AHM Publishing Corporation, 1978.

Seiler, J. A. "Diagnosing Interdepartmental Conflict." *Harvard Business Review,* 41 (September-October 1963): 121-132.

Sherif, M. "Experiments in Group Conflict." *Scientific American* 195 (1956): 54-58.

Simon, H. A. "On the Concept of Organizational Goal." *Administrative Science Quarterly* 9 (June 1964): 1-22.

Thompson, J. D. *Organizations in Action.* New York: McGraw-Hill, 1967.

3

Coalitions and Cliques

Coalitions, cliques, cabals—these and other informal social entities form, grow, alter, and vanish in all organizations. Sometimes these groupings are very powerful in influencing an organization's processes; sometimes they develop merely to satisfy needs for human companionship. Although it is not possible to distinguish among the various grouping possibilities in a precise and definitive manner, we will attempt to highlight the differences in formation, motivation, and structure for the primary informal groups. They are of interest to study, whether one is a manager seeking to control or cope with them, a worker seeking to join or organize one, or a theoretician seeking to understand human social phenomena. Later in the chapter I will explain more fully the impact these informal social groupings have upon various areas of the organization.

THEORIES OF FORMATION METHODS

This chapter is addressed to the consideration of those members of an organization who stand apart from the organization (psychologically) and band together to achieve some ulterior purpose.

DEFINITIONS: If the purpose is to gain control over (part of) the organization's resources, this is usually referred to as a *coalition*.

If the banding together is patently proscribed or if the people in question are not supposed to have control over the resources in question, then this grouping is typically called a *cabal*.

If the banding together merely occurs for reasons of social support, friendship, having a good time together, and so on, this group is commonly called a *clique*.

If the banding together is officially constituted by the organization (e.g., as a committee or a work group), it is called a *formal group*. Coalitions, cabals, and cliques are *informal groups*.

Parts of all these definitions may characterize any one real social group found in an actual organization. We shall loosely treat all as being variants on the one central theme, occasionally focusing on a particular group to the exclusion of the others.

There are several classes of theories which purport to explain how informal groups arise in organizations. Some theories examine the psychological characteristics of the participants. Other theories are much more oriented toward "political science" or "economics," devoting most of their attention to the bargaining that goes on. Yet other theories place greater emphasis upon the organizational milieu in which the people behave.

PSYCHOLOGICAL THEORIES

Homans (1950) feels that people who interact frequently or who engage in common activities will soon come to develop positive sentiments toward one another; that is, an informal on-the-job group will develop. One supposes that the greater the social needs, such as the needs to cope with failure, to achieve control or dominance, or the needs for affiliation, the more rapidly will this process ensue. If this interaction-activity-sentiment pattern is disrupted or if new individual needs emerge, there will be a shift in the once-stable informal group. But if the group is stable for long enough, a new set of sentiments will emerge from the interaction of the group members. These new sentiments are called *norms*, which are informal rules, serving to prescribe and proscribe acceptable patterns of behavior for all "good" members of this informal group (see Kiesler, 1978, for more detailed information on groups and norms).

There are other primarily psychological theories of informal grouping built upon the notion of "exchange." That is, when two people discover they would both be better off by giving up something they have to the other person, or sharing, a basis for an exchange system is established (see Gergen, 1969). For example, one person may be willing to do part of another person's work in trade for public praise from him or for having him relate amusing stories. Or one person may discover he is inept at task t_1 and the other person may really prefer not to do task t_2; again, a trade may be in order. The exchange theories focus upon how "distributive justice" (see Homans, 1961) and "equity" (see Adams, 1965) are perceived and what steps are taken once an imbalance is sensed (see Thibaut and Kelley, 1959).

POLITICAL SCIENCE/ECONOMICS/ BARGAINING THEORIES

Whereas the psychological class of theories addressed all types of groupings, this class is primarily concerned with coalitions and cabals. The interest is to control the organization's resources. What awaits the members of the winning group is some resource prize unavailable to the members individually and which is greater than a simple pooling of the resources each alone commands. Coalition theorists explain the formation of coalitions by reference to one primary variable: the initial distribution of power (or some surrogate, e.g., resources at one's own personal command), across those vying for a position in the coalition. That the S-R paradigm underlies this conception of how coalitions form should be readily apparent. This viewpoint is too narrow ever to be completely successful; there are simply too many other factors of importance (e.g., the communication network, each person's bargaining ability independent of the resources he commands). However, it seems sensible to study carefully the effects of one factor (power) upon the phenomenon of interest (coalition formation) while controlling for the other factors, so we will begin there. (The concept of power is more thoroughly discussed in Simmons, 1978.)

One such theory might be called the "maximum control" theory (see Caplow, 1956). Imagine a triad (three persons), any two of whom have sufficient total power to control. Call the three persons A, B, and C. Suppose that the relative power distribution is such that $A > B > C$ where $x > y$ means "x has more power than y" or "x has power over y" and $(B + C) > A$. (Note: Since $A > B > C$, we ignore the two uninteresting cases, $(A + B) > C$ and $(A + C) > B$.) According to Caplow, each person selects the coalition that maximizes the number of people he controls ("controls" in the sense of "more power than"). Consider the three possible coalitions (*AB*, *AC*, *BC*) from the three perspectives of *A*, *B*, and C.

A—dislikes *BC*, but is indifferent between *AB* and *AC* since in either case he controls two persons (the coalition controls the person excluded and, because *A* > *B* > *C*, *A* controls whichever other person is in the coalition.

B—dislikes *AC*, and prefers the *BC* coalition to the *AB* coalition (in *AB*, *B* only controls *C*; in *BC*, *B* controls both *A* and *C*).

C—dislikes *AB*, and is indifferent between *AC* and *AB* (since in either case he only controls the excluded person).

This analysis shows that *B* will never seek out *A* as a coalition partner; thus only coalitions *AC* and *BC* are possible. If persons *A* and *C* are truly indifferent as to whom their partners are, then coalitions *AC* and *BC* are equally likely to occur. (Given *B*'s strength of preference for *C* some, e.g., Chertkoff, 1967, have reformulated the last assumption so *BC* is more likely than *AC* to occur.)

It is interesting to note that Caplow's "maximum control" theory runs completely counter to a commonly employed heuristic argument: To get ahead, join forces with the boss and ride his coattails. It is not clear if this rule of thumb casts doubt on Caplow's theory or whether it points out the lack of rationality of status aspirants and power seekers.

Since in the usual bargaining theory of coalition formation the primary explanatory variable is the initial distribution of power or resources, a complete theory must consider all of the cases of possible power distribution. For the triad, this means the cases such as *A* = *B* = *C* (any coalition is possible), *A* > (*B* + *C*) (no coalition is possible), *A* > *B*, *B* = *C*, *A* < (*B* + *C*) (only coalition *BC* is possible), and so on. Of such theories, Caplow (1968) has probably the most definitive study of triads; he not only examines triadic coalition formation in organizations, but also in family and other kinship units, in *Hamlet*, in the monkey and ape primates, and through the span of history, including political parties, classes, and nations!

Another theory requires that the amount of power or resources brought to the coalition be measured because the distribution of the overall prize will be made proportionally to the resources brought (thus the resources measure the demands made on the prize). Gamson's (1961) "minimum resource" theory argues that the coalition which will form is the one which is smallest in total resources (since each person, by assumption, seeks to maximize his share of the prize and since, by further assumption, the parity norm is in effect and the prize is divided in proportion to resources). For example, assume another triad in which A brings six units of power, B five, C four, and a total of nine units is needed to obtain rights to the prize of $990. The usual notation for such situations is "total power needed: power of person 1, power of person 2, . . . , power of person n." Thus the standard notation for this particular situation is "9 : 6, 5, 4." Again consider the three possible coalitions as viewed by the three participants.

A—gets $0 from the BC coalition, and from the AB coalition gets $990 x 6/(5 + 6) = $990 x 6/11 = $540. From AC he gets $990 x 6/10 = $594. He clearly prefers the AC coalition.

B—gets $0 from AC, gets $990 x 5/(5 + 6) = $990 x 5/11 = $450 from AB, and gets $990 x 5/9 = $550 from BC. He obviously prefers BC.

C—gets $0 from AB, gets $990 x 4/10 = $396 from AC, and gets $990 x 4/9 = $440 from BC. He naturally prefers BC.

Since two persons prefer the identical coalition (BC), they seek each other out and only that coalition forms, no others. Note that in the example, as required by Gamson's minimum resource theory, the coalition with smallest total resources (BC, with nine units of power) is the one that occurs.

A third theory is due to Shapley and Shubik (1954) in which they argue that the crucial concept is that of "pivotal power," which measures the proportion of time that each person's resources are pivotal in their ability to convert a losing coalition into a winning one. The Shapley and Shubik theory is an example of N-person game theory; see Luce and Raiffa (1957). Mathematical N-person game theory (with $N \geq 3$) has only tangential relevance for the study of coalition formation since its orientation is normative; that is, it indicates how individuals should optimally behave in that situation.

Komorita and Chertkoff (1973) have developed a theory of coalition formation which focuses upon the bargaining process which ensues. Partly because they incorporate some notions of process and partly because they are not restricted to the triad, their theory appears to be superior to all other extant coalition formation theories. In their theory, there are three important phases that occur: prenegotiation, first encounter, and subsequent encounters. In the prenegotiation phase, all individuals form expectations about the outcomes that they will acquire from each of the winning coalitions that are possible. Individuals relatively strong in resources (power) advocate the parity norm (split the prize proportionally with resources) whereas those relatively weak in power advocate the equality norm (all N people in the coalition each receive $1/N$ of the prize). Everyone's expectations, then, are halfway between the best and the worst (one-half of what he could expect under parity plus equality). Each person then is predisposed toward that coalition which maximizes his expected split of the prize. (Parenthetically, some of these assumptions strain reality in order to produce a tractable model, i.e., that the "only" source of power is from the resources, and that people are capable of quickly calculating their split of the prize under equality, parity, and most likely expectation.)

In the first encounter phase, bargaining occurs and negotiations progress; those who

are resource-rich offer parity, the others
hold out for equality. However, should there
be pressure on anyone to reach agreement, the
greater the deviation of the initial offer
from the best he could hope for to what he
legitimately expects, the faster the concession rate. From this negotiation process, a
winning coalition eventually emerges.

In the subsequent encounter phase, individuals not members of winning coalitions are
likely to concede more than those present in
the coalitions. Furthermore, the longer the
time a person is excluded, the greater the
concession rate. A person *in* a winning coalition will be more tempted to defect to a
countercoalition the more his share of the
prize deviates from what he could expect in an
alternative coalition. The greater an offer
to defect is above what outcome the person is
enjoying in the current coalition, the more
likely he is to defect. Finally, the stability
of a coalition is an inverse function of the
degree to which its individual members are
tempted to defect.

Komorita and Chertkoff have performed some
modest empirical tests of their theory, finding, for example, that they could predict both
the winning coalitions and the split of the
prize better than either Shapley and Shubik's
pivotal power theory or Gamson's minimum resource theory (but of course theirs did not
predict perfectly). However, it should be
noted that neither they nor anyone else has
yet reported empirical tests of the bargaining
process that is so central to their theory. It
is the process part of their theory which significantly differentiates it from other theories of coalition formation. Furthermore, the
process part of their theory is mainly lodged
in the bargaining phase, and the activities
they posit ring echoes that sound like conventional economics—calculation of marginal
physical productivity of rewards, movement
away from a disequilibrium position to an

equilibrium position of a set of stable coalitions, and so on.

ORGANIZATIONAL MILIEU THEORIES

There are a number of factors, peculiar to
organizational environments, which can cause
or hasten the formation of informal social
groups. For example, strong identification
with a subunit or a subgoal (more thoroughly
discussed in the previous chapter) can lead
to a clique or a cabal in order to facilitate
the achievement of the unit's purposes or to
further the relative intraorganizational power
of the unit. Whatever is obtained (clique or
cabal) depends upon the nature of the subunit's
goals and whether it is possible to satisfy
them through legitimate actions.

Another factor is the perceived relative
deprivation of one set of members of the organization as compared to some other set of
members. The greater the deprivation, the
greater the inner pressure of those members
who perceive themselves to be deprived (e.g.,
of sharing in rewards—money, status, authority, etc.) to form cliques or cabals to "rectify" the situation.

A third factor is in some sense the reverse
of the previous one. Cliques sometimes form to
perpetuate inequitous status, reward, and
authority systems, among others. Often, one
finds that cliques crystallize around common
task-oriented behaviors. If you were to survey
the lunchroom of a large firm, for example, you
would probably find that the managers eat by
themselves, the foremen sit together separately
from all the others, the workers have an area
identified as belonging to them, and so on.
You would probably also find that people will
sit with their "own" group and initiate interactions with them, even though they have never
met before.

Perhaps the most carefully constructed theory
of clique and cabal formation is due to Tichy

(1973). He explains their formation by reference to three variables: mobility, compliance, and size. The size variable is obvious (the number of members in an organization) but the other two require some explanation. Tichy's mobility variable is derived from Gumpert and Smith's (1968) definitions of three kinds of mobility systems. In the "high-mobility" system, promotion is based primarily upon merit, and meritorious individuals advance fairly rapidly. In the "seniority" system, promotion is due largely to length of time on the job. In the "no-mobility" system, promotion never occurs.

Tichy's compliance variable is based upon the typology of power developed by Etzioni (1961). In Etzioni's formulation, organizations fit into differing categories according to the means employed to make their members comply. The three types of compliance systems are (1) coercive, in which physical threat is used (e.g., as in total organizations such as prisons—the authorities coerce the prisoners); (2) utilitarian, in which material resources are disbursed (e.g., as in business firms); and (3) normative, in which symbolic rewards are allocated and manipulated (e.g., as in voluntary organizations such as the Boy Scouts or a rural fire department, but also including hospitals and colleges).

Tichy uses these three variables to explain the formation of five types of informal groups —(1) coercive, (2) normative, (3) high-mobility utilitarian, (4) seniority utilitarian, and (5) no-mobility utilitarian. He also explains each group's structural characteristics and motivational base (reason for formation), although his explanation assumes a static formal structure and is largely drawn from the S-R paradigm.

The coercive type of informal group forms for two reasons: (1) The members seek to gain counterpower since they are usually in open conflict with the formal organization, and (2) they seek mutual aid and support in coping with their alienation from the formal organization and the hostile environment it presents to them. Generally, only the lower-level members of coercive organizations are part of the coercive cliques and cabals, but virtually all lower members are part of one. Occupational categories (e.g., the kitchen, library, hospital, and garden details) tend to have little effect on which groupings occur. Frequently, there are a small number of such groupings in an organization, with each one being moderately large (in membership), mostly closed (people only have relationships with members of the same clique), and fairly well differentiated (with respect to its internal authority structure).

Members of normative cliques have most of their needs met in the formal work setting, since the members of normative organizations tend to be professionals. Therefore, the formal work groups and the normative cliques overlap to a considerable extent. Such cliques form to satisfy the omnipresent and apparently insatiable human needs of friendship and affiliation. The cliques tend to be small, the better to satisfy the intimate needs of friendship, but open (there are many ties and relationships outside the cliques). Organizational size has a modest effect upon normative cliques: the larger the organization, the more work groups there are, and so the more normative cliques there are (and conversely). There is little by way of internal clique hierarchy.

High-mobility utilitarian social groupings have but one purpose: getting ahead, and the relationships that develop are the means to that end. The lower-status members of those groups tend to be thought of as "apprentices"; the higher-status members are "patrons." Advancement of the juniors occurs, at least in part, from patrons negotiating with other influential seniors. The lower-status people need to join such cliques to learn the intricate patterns of higher-status behavior, appropriate attitudes, task expertise, and so on,

and to receive advancement. Higher-status members are judged, at least partially, on their
ability to bring good men up through the system. As such, a relatively high proportion of
people in such organizations belongs to a high-
mobility utilitarian group. The larger the organization, the smaller that proportion is.
The reason is that in small organizations,
isolated individuals are very visible, whereas
in large organizations, it is easier for isolated individuals to go unnoticed and uninflu-
enced by such groups and to advance on their
own. It is also true that the larger the organization, the smaller the dispersion of
ranks present in any one group. And even though
these groups tend to be relatively open (people often solicit "useful" friendships), they
are even more open when the organization is
smaller.

Seniority utilitarian cliques form, not out
of competition over promotion, but from the
needs for friendship and affiliation that
emerge with the lack of instrumental pressure.
There are generally a moderate number of such
cliques, each of moderate size, each with its
own modest structure (higher-status being related more to seniority than competence), and
each being moderately open.

In no-mobility utilitarian organizations,
members eventually resign themselves to accept
and be satisfied with the position in which
they are "stuck." Since the no-mobility participant is in a very stable environment (no
need to learn new task procedures or groom for
a new role), and since "misery loves company"
(but only if it is suffering from comparable
misery), the cliques that do form are often
from the same status level within the organization; and the reasons for forming are usually
to commiserate and satisfy friendship and affiliation needs. Such cliques tend to be
large, so the larger the organization from
which to draw members, the larger the cliques.
Even though large, these cliques do not tend
to be very differentiated. Like coercive

cliques, no-mobility utilitarian cliques are
generally closed—their members interact only
with others from the same clique. Since he
cannot advance, why should the member look
elsewhere for friendships?

PROCESS THEORIES

Rudimentary process models of cliques and
coalition formation are sketched in this section; since cabals may be thought of as secretive coalitions, they will not be treated separately. Because of the preliminary nature of
these models, they have not yet been empirically tested. However, because they build upon
the theories from the first three sections and
because they correct some of the deficiencies
of those previous theories, their credibility
should be relatively high.

People continually seek out other people
that are similar to themselves, where "similar"
may mean any or all of the following charac-
tersitics: comparable values, comparable career
goals, comparable life experiences, comparable
educational backgrounds, comparable attitudes,
opinions, biases and outlooks, comparable age
and socioeconomic status, comparable political
and religious philosophies, comparable recreational interests, comparable occupation or work
activities, comparable conversational interests, and, in general, a degree of "liking"
and/or "loving" for one another. The greater
the number of these similarities that hold
true, the greater the affinity for and cohesion of the grouping. When the grouping occurs
within the boundaries of a formal organization,
it is called a clique, but such groupings also
occur outside of the typical formal organization: There are kinship systems (the decision
of A and B to get married is an instance of
an extra-organizational clique), good friends,
clubs, interest groups, alumni associations,
social organizations, fraternal organizations,
neighborhood coffee groups, brown-bag-to-lunch-
bunches, and so on.

People seek out others similar to themselves
for a variety of reasons. Man is a social ani-
mal of course, so there are always unfulfilled
social needs. Although strictly speaking *anyone*
could satisfy a person's social needs (by carrying on his end of the interaction) usually
just any person will not do. Instead, people
turn to their golfing partner or their bridge
partner or their coin collecting partner, and
so on, when they are looking for someone to go
to the movies with, have over for dinner, or
go along for drinks. To satisfy their social
needs, people seek out others who speak with
the same working vocabulary, who have had
similar experiences to draw upon for examples
and proofs of arguments, who have the same out-
look and philosophy of life (whether precisely
articulated or not), and who will support their
cluster of attitudes.

Because people change—they learn new things,
their attitudes shift, old interests expire and
new ones arise, and so on—cliques are rarely
stable. People continually search for new or
expanded clique associations. Sometimes, the
searching is passive—when new acquaintances
are made (e.g., a new person joins your work
crew, or a friend introduces a friend of his),
the other person is "sized up" for his degree
of similarity. As interactions continue and as
each person continues to be judged similar
enough, more details of each person's attitudes, values, experiences, and so on, may be
revealed. However, different people are con-
fided in (and different types of support are
sought from them) to various degrees on a wide
range of issues. Sometimes, the searching is
active; for example, the person joins a club
or subscribes to a specialized publication.
As new acquaintances are made, they are also
subjected to the scrutinizing process.

If the scrutinizing process progresses far
enough, that is, when sufficient detail has
been traded so that a feeling of closeness or
intimacy is achieved, a clique has been developed. But because the scrutinizing process

unfolds in small units over a prolonged time
period, there is not the either/or case of no
clique/clique. Instead, people are in various
degrees of "cliqueiness" with their acquaintances at all times. (But to keep things simple, we will continue to refer to cliques as
those social units which enjoy a relatively
high degree of intermember friendship.)

In distinction from cliques, coalitions arise
to effect change in some sector of the organization where there is an authority vacuum. (If
authority governs that arena, one speaks of a
cabal arising.) This encompasses two types of
reasons for coalition formation: First, to try
to rectify some problematic situation, probably
a recurring one, and second, the opportunity to
obtain sufficient power to wield control over
some of the organization's resources. As an
example of the first case, consider the plight
of a group of people who are maneuvering to remove a disliked but competent department head
from his office; for the second case, consider
the question of where a new computer installa-
tion will be located within the structure of
the organization. In both of these examples,
at least one and probably more coalitions will
unite in trying to bring about the changes.

Whenever either of these two conditions exist
(clearly visible intraorganizational problems
or opportunities) and whenever individual people feel that they could have a greater impact
upon the decision collectively rather than individually, coalitions will form. Next, consider the question of who appears in which
coalitions. For each issue (problem or opportunity) that arises, there will be a small
number of core people around whom the coalitions will form. The core people are those who
are directly affected by the issue, or are the
most forceful, or have the highest energy levels for advocating their position on the issue.
If all the core people agree on the issue,
only one coalition will form; but as some of the
core people disagree with one another, a number of
alternative, competing coalitions will form.

Once the core people and coalition possibilities have been identified, coalitions' member-
ships are built up by the core people who recruit for their own coalitions. The people
sought out for membership by a core person must
satisfy three conditions:

1. They must be homogeneous with respect to the
   issues behind the formation of the coalition.
2. They must bring power or resources to the
   coalition.
3. They must be able to derive some benefit
   from being in the coalition.

Because of those three necessary conditions,
core people often turn to members of their own
cliques for possible recruitees into their
coalitions. The outcome of this process is usually observed as follows: When problems or opportunities arise in organizations, cliques
often crystallize into coalitions.

When a person is considering joining a coalition, there is typically a round of bargaining that occurs between him and the recruiter
as to what he will be expected to contribute
and how he can expect to benefit. (See the
inducements-contributions analysis of the decision to participate in a group, March and
Simon, 1958, ch. 4.) The greater the resources
or power that he commands, or the more his
power or resources are needed, the greater is
his bargaining advantage. But, the greater the
benefits he can receive, or the greater the
current membership of the coalition, the lesser
his bargaining advantage is. Finally, it should
be recognized that some people are better bar-
gainers than others—some have a reputation for
meeting promises, other for breaking them; some
have power bases beyond resources and authority
commanded (e.g., expertise, charisma); some
have greater experience at bargaining, greater
interpersonal skill, greater tact, greater
ability to be subtle, devious, and so on.

Once coalitions have formed, the activities
of the core people shift somewhat. Their main

task is to keep the coalition stable, build solidarity, and increase commitment. This is done by making adjustments at the margin in contributions extracted from the members and in inducements offered them (e.g., modifications in the side payments offered). Some effort is also made to clarify the advantages of membership in the coalition.

Regarding defection from a coalition, Komorita and Chertkoff (1973) have presented what is probably the best statement of how that process occurs, albeit a neoeconomic theory.

Armed with these theories of how cliques and coalitions form, grow, alter, and die, now consider the areas of organizational behavior upon which they have an impact.

AREAS AFFECTED

As you have seen, one of the most frequent determinants of a clique is its ability to satisfy social needs. It is also, undoubtedly, a significant factor in the formation of cabals, coalitions, and other informal social groupings; to a considerable extent, people disregard the outcome and are merely happy to be part of the game of "the ins and the outs." But besides maintaining people's mental health and happiness (your group is a place to relax, a place to blow off anger and vent frustration at the system, your boss, etc.), these social groups can have an important impact on many formal areas of an organization's existence and well-being. The influence that cliques, cabals, and coalitions have on five such areas will be sketched: (1) goals and objectives, (2) the problems that are attended to, (3) the reward and task systems, (4) the decision-making processes, and (5) productivity and efficiency.

GOALS AND OBJECTIVES

As discussed in chapter 2, the coalition that forms (at the top of the organization) can have

a significant impact on what the operative
goals and objectives will be. Since different
people have different personal values and different organizational backgrounds, it is not
surprising that when new people enter the dominant coalition, the organization's goals will
probably change.

However, both cliques and cabals can affect
goals. Once the existence of cabals is discovered, the higher echelons in the organization may take steps (i.e., institute goals) to
eliminate such groups in general or just the
particular ones they know of (e.g., reassign-
ing people), or to minimize their potential
effectiveness (e.g., to take steps that change
the conditions which caused the formation of
the cabal). In any case, many organizations
are on the lookout for cabals developing, and
formulate internal goals (policies) to cope
with those situations.

As noted in Kiesler (1978), it is unusual for
any group, be it a coalition, clique, or cabal,
to develop without it forming its own "norms"—
internal guidelines for its own members' behaviors. The norms also behave as operative, if
sometimes illegitimate, goals—at least for the
members of the group in question—and if the
group ever becomes dominantly powerful, its
members can enforce their norms across the organization.

Cliques which develop at the top of an organization will influence its goals since the
members of the clique can be more frank and
open in discussing problems, prospects, true
feelings, and so on. Those not a member of a
particular clique are more cautious and defensive in their interactions with others at
the top of the organization.

Cliques which arise at lower levels of the
organization can also affect goals if they become so satisfying that their members prefer
being in them to working for an organization;
that is, they can be counter-productive. In
those (fortunately few) cases, other internal
goals and policies must be developed so the

necessary work of the organization is accomplished.

PROBLEMS ATTENDED TO

The members of the winning dominant coalition, and other ruling coalitions throughout the organization, clearly have a strong say in which problems are attended to. As just noted, certain cliques and cabals may be interpreted as being problems in their own right. However, they also have a broader impact on the set of problems to which the organization pays attention. In chapters 4 and 6, I will consider a broader range of the spectrum of possible problem types and search mechanisms. As you will then see, the set of SOPs can be altered, and the use of reactive and opportunistic search can be increased, because the members of winning or dominant coalitions, cabals, and cliques typically have some set of burning issues with which they enter office. However, intense bursts of problem-solving activity are usually limited to the focal issues or other important problems which arise during their reign.

When cabals proliferate, not only do they pose a problem to the organization, but their existence is also symbolic and symptomatic of some deeper problems that may need attention. People do not band together to seek counter-power in a vacuum; something stimulates them to do it.

Cliques, by their very relaxed, often intimate nature, permit greater freedom of expression. One result may be that more problems are disclosed, problems that may be personal, or due to a personal blunder, or whose solution is unlikely to advance anyone's career. In the absence of cliques, these problems are not likely to be revealed. But with cliques, they may be presented in hopes that a friendly, constructive solution to them may be found.

REWARD AND TASK SYSTEMS

The dominant coalition can obviously determine what the organization's reward system will be like while it holds power (what will be rewarded, what the rate will be, who will be singled out, what special projects will be funded, etc.). However, to the extent that other coalitions or cabals gain significant power, they can modify the reward system used by the dominant coalition.

Cliques have relatively little impact upon the reward system, except for those cliques to which members of powerful coalitions or cabals belong. In those cliques, special interest can be levered through friendship to persons who are members of the powerful coalitions. In this way oblique control or influence is possible.

It should also be noted that it is very rewarding to be a member of a clique, cabal, or coalition, and it is even more rewarding to be a member of a dominant one. For most, this is so rewarding that there is no need to affect changes in the formal reward system except to ensure compliance with the new group's desires for organizational performance.

With the presence of cliques, coalitions, or cabals, or with changes in their membership, the task system and the way work gets done can be drastically altered. As these proliferate and diminish in number and size, the steps necessary to complete tasks change. Mackenzie (1978) discusses these effects on structure, and Pfeffer (1978) examines the impact of these groups when considering the question of organizational design.

DECISION-MAKING PROCESSES

The coalitions which develop affect the decision-making processes. The larger the coalitions, or the more nearly equal the power in a coalition, the more people with whom a given decision situation must be checked out. The

particular people present in a coalition will
affect the range of alternatives considered,
how the decision situation is defined, what
the evaluation function is, and the manner in
which the chosen alternative is implemented
(for more information on how individuals make
decision, see Jabes, 1978). Coalitions also
obviously modify the decision-making processes
when they redesign the organization or alter
its goals and objectives (see ch. 4 on standard operating procedures).

The presence of cliques can influence the
decision-making processes since the decision
situations can be more openly, honestly, and
thoroughly investigated and discussed. Furthermore, their informal status and authority systems may not correspond with those of the organization.

PRODUCTIVITY AND EFFICIENCY

Productivity is largely a function of ability
and incentives (see ch. 2 of Simmons, 1978 for
a more detailed discussion), but there are those
who argue (see Roethlisberger and Dickson, 1939)
that the work groups, in particular the cliques,
have a much stronger effect. Usually what is
studied is the norms of those groups, especially
norms of output restriction or diminished efficiency. For example, it has been found that the
more cohesive those informal groups are, the
more effective the norms are at controlling the
behaviors of individual members of those groups.
However, occasionally one finds cliques with
organizationally oriented productivity norms
(e.g., high research output departments in
universities).

The presence of cabals and coalitions also
detracts from productivity and efficiency since
the time spent in meeting, negotiating, and
plotting is lost to the organization. As noted
in chapter 9, intraorganizational conflict usually detracts from efficiency and effectiveness.
As coalitions vie for dominance and as cabals
combat the formal system, conflict and strife
are present, ergo detracting from the efficiency
and effectiveness of the system.

In conclusion, I have tried to explain in this chapter several theories, only some of which are well substantiated empirically, of how coalitions, cliques, and cabals form. I have also indicated several important areas of organizational existence that they affect—areas where they are assumed not to have any influence, but in fact they do.

REFERENCES

Adams, J. S. "Inequity in Social Exchange." In *Advances in Experimental Social Psychology*, edited by L. Berkowitz, vol. 2. New York: Academic Press, 1965.

Caplow, T. "A Theory of Coalitions in the Triad." *American Sociological Review* 21 (1956): 489-493.

_____. *Two Against One: Coalitions in Triads*. Englewood Cliffs, N.J.: Prentice-Hall, 1968.

Chertkoff, J. M. "A Revision of Caplow's Coalition Theory." *Journal of Experimental Social Psychology* 3 (1967): 172-177.

Etzioni, A. *A Comparative Analysis of Complex Organizations*. New York: Macmillan, 1961.

Gamson, W. A. "A Theory of Coalition Formation." *American Sociological Review* 26 (1961): 373-382.

Gergen, K. J. *The Psychology of Behavior Exchange*. Reading, Mass.: Addison-Wesley, 1969.

Gumpert, P., and Smith, W. National Science Foundation research proposal, mimeographed. New York: Teacher's College at Columbia University, 1968.

Homans, G. C. *The Human Group*. New York: Harcourt, Brace and World, 1950.

_____. *Social Behavior: Its Elementary Forms*. New York: Harcourt, Brace and World, 1961.

Jabes, J. *Individual Processes in Organizational Behavior*. Arlington Heights, Ill.: AHM Publishing Corporation, 1978.

Kiesler, S. *Interpersonal Processes in Groups and Organizations*. Arlington Heights, Ill.: AHM Publishing Corporation, 1978.

Komorita, S. S., and Chertkoff, J. M. "A Bargaining Theory of Coalition Formation." *Psychological Review* 80, no. 3 (May 1973): 149-162.

Luce, R. D., and Raiffa, H. *Games and Decisions*. New York: Wiley, 1957.

Mackenzie, K. D. *Organizational Structures*. Arlington Heights, Ill.: AHM Publishing Corporation, 1978.

March, J. G., and Simon, H. A. *Organizations*. New York: Wiley, 1958.

Pfeffer, J. *Organizational Design*. Arlington Heights, Ill.: AHM Publishing Corporation, 1978.

Roethlisberger, F., and Dickson, W. J. *Management and the Worker*. Cambridge, Mass.: Harvard University Press, 1939.

Shapley, L. S., and Shubik, M. "A Method for Evaluating the Distribution of Power in a Committee System." *American Political Science Review* 48 (1954): 787-792.

Simmons, R. E. *Managing Behavioral Processes: Applications of Theory and Research*. Arlington Heights, Ill.: AHM Publishing Corporation, 1978.

Thibaut, J. W., and Kelley, H. H. *The Social Psychology of Groups*. New York: Wiley, 1959.

Tichy, N. "An Analysis of Clique Formation and Structure in Organizations." *Administrative Science Quarterly* 18, no. 2 (June 1973): 194-208.

4

Standard Operating Procedures

Organizations are confronted by a bewildering variety of problems, of greater and lesser degrees of importance. Some problems recur, some occur only one time. Some problems are broad and involve many segments of the organization, and others are narrow. Examples of organizational problems include:

1. What happens when inventory runs low?
2. What goes on after a person resigns from the organization?
3. Should the organization continue to process paperwork manually, or should it buy, or lease, a computer?
4. When more warehouse space is needed, where should it be located?
5. How should products, or services, be priced?
6. What should be done after there is an accident in which someone is injured?

7. In which markets should the organizations be competing?

In order to describe organizational behavior in reaction to problems in a coherent fashion, we shall need to examine some definitions and to recognize that problems, and decision problems, are *always* present in any organization.

DEFINITION: A *problem* is a state of the organization with which one or more members of the organization are dissatisfied. Note that the state causing the dissatisfaction can be a past state, a current state, a projected or likely future state, or a possible future state. The dissatisfaction necessarily means that there is a preferred, or less "bad," state envisioned. The problem-solving process consists of inventing, selecting, and testing a sequence of operators to remove that undesirable difference.

DEFINITION: A *decision problem* is a situation that ultimately requires a selection between a number of action alternatives. The major reason for decision-making is to try to find actions that transform an unacceptable state into an acceptable one. Of course, since the different people in an organization hold dissimilar perceptions, values, goals, and so on, the organization is never entirely problem-free: What person A views as an acceptable state may dissatisfy person B.

DEFINITION: A *problematic situation* is any case that involves either a problem to be solved or a decision to be made. In this chapter, some of the important features of problematic situations are first introduced, so that standard operating procedures (SOPs) can be properly discussed, the material on organizational problem-solving in chapter 6 can be understood, and the relationship between these bodies of knowledge can be appreciated. (For other views on problems and problem-solving, see Kiesler, 1978; for decision problems, see Jabes, 1978.)

We have to recognize that at the heart of it, all problematic situations in an organization are interconnected, although for an arbitrary pair of them (inventory stockout and a personnel termination in the marketing area, for example) the web of connection may be thin. (In the example case, the stockout affects working capital and the turnover affects the marketing activities which will eventually affect the revenues produced, so both have some tiny effect upon the profit function for the firm.) In a similar vein, a decision made in one part of the organization may engender problems for some other parts of the organization; however, the induced problems may be relatively insignificant and may be much removed in time and space. In spite of the facts that *some* sets of problems are tightly interconnected (which markets to enter? what prices to charge?) and that *some* solutions induce other problems immediately, people in organizations tend to treat problematic situations in isolation from one another. (For example, to replace inefficient equipment with faster operating equipment implies at a minimum these types of changes, or potential problems: Inventory builds up faster, material and supplies will be needed at a higher rate, and many people will have to be re-instructed or retrained--equipment operators, suppliers, and inventory handlers.)

There are several reasons for this behavior. It is simpler and imposes less cognitive strain than seeking out all of the interconnections and interdependencies. People are very busy and may not have the time to search. We know that people are limited in their information-processing capabilities (Simon, 1957, pp. 196ff, calls this condition "bounded rationality"), and so the interrelationships may fail to be discovered. It may also be felt that the related or implied problems are someone else's responsibility. There is great respect for organizational division.

DIMENSIONS OF PROBLEMATIC SITUATIONS

Two characteristics of organizational problematic situations are most fruitful for analysis: the degree of familiarity with the situation (as perceived by the person coping with it) and its time horizon (also subjective). Each feature is a continuum, but it is common to focus attention upon the endpoints of each dimension—routine/novel in the former case, and static/continuing in the latter.

Routine problematic situations are those with which a person is completely familiar: They are standard, stable, for the most part well defined and unchanging, and there is a well-known history of dealing with them. (Recall, this is an ideal type, the endpoint of a continuum.) Problematic situations which fit this description, or that are ascribed to lie in this portion of the continuum, can be handled by a previously developed set of rules. These rules are called *standard operating procedures* or SOPs. An intriguing fact about SOPs is their pervasiveness; most organizations view most of their problematic situations as fitting into this category.

At the opposite end of the familiarity continuum, novel situations are those which the focal person has never encountered before, and for which he has not learned a solution procedure. These situations require the usual behavioral steps called problem-solving (e.g., generation and testing of hypotheses) and/or decision-making (e.g., generating alternatives, formulating a choice procedure, making a choice). People in organizations attempt to avoid these situations, usually by treating them as familiar or routine, and by evoking some SOP. There are several reasons for this: Novel situations are stressful; SOPs can be executed rapidly; there exists organizational approval for SOPs; and pure problem-solving and decision-making steps may fail, may consume much time, and over-identify the person with the results of the process (in the extreme, one may put the person's career on the line).

Another useful feature to take into account when considering familiarity with a situation is the degree of "programmedness" of the solution procedure. SOPs are sometimes referred to as completely programmed procedures, and pure problem-solving is sometimes referred to as a completely unprogrammed procedure (see March and Simon, 1958, pp. 141ff).

Concerning the other dimension of time horizon, some problems are static, that is, what they concern is abruptly delimited in time. (This too is a hypothetical endpoint of a continuum.) Static problematic situations concern some phenomenon that is temporally delimited, but this definition does not preclude the frequent recurrence of the phenomenon. For example, when some production equipment breaks down, this situation will probably recur in the future; but once the particular problem is solved, it is no longer attended to—it is bounded in time. For another example of a static novel decision problem, consider the case of a firm that for the first time in its history must choose a site for a new warehouse. Situations of the static type are amenable to ordinary solution methods, whether they be of the SOP type (for static routine situations) or of the unprogrammed type (for static novel situations).

At the other end of the time horizon continuum is the continuing problem, one whose scope includes the current state of the organization forward into perpetuity. Methods used for situations with this feature are variously labelled—continuing routine situations are solved through *planning*; continuing novel situations are called either *policy making* (if the substance of the problem concerns internal operation of the firm) or *strategy formulation* (if the situation concerns the firm's relations with its environment, market, industry, or another external entity).

In the next several paragraphs, I will develop and explain propositions relating several of the concepts introduced thus far in this chapter. The rationale for each proposition is to be found in an informal process model of the behaviors it addresses. Formal process models are lacking for the usual reason of insufficient development of the field. Do note the richness of even informal process models— a large number of propositions could be derived from each such model, formalized, and tested.

PROPOSITION: The lower echelons in an organization devote a higher proportion of their time to static routine situations than do the higher echelons in an organization. Similarly, as one increases the level of focus within an organization, the relative proportion of time spent on novel continuing situations increases. The other two types of situations (static novel and continuing routine) tend to be solved in the middle layers of the organization. Stated differently, the lower units spend a greater proportion of their time executing SOPs, the middle layers monitoring and adapting SOPS, and engaged in some problem-solving, and the higher units setting policy and designing strategy. Thus the process evoked for coping with a situation and the types of situations considered vary as the strata in the organization. (Thompson and Tuden, 1959, offer a related proposition which connects the levels of agreement about goals and the causes of the problem to the decision strategies and organizational structures adopted for the different types of issues: When there is agreement about both goals and causes, computation occurs in bureaucratic structures; when there is agreement on causes but disagreement on goals, bargaining in representative structures; agreement on goals but disagreement on causes, majority judgment in collegial structures; and disagreement on both, inspiration in "anomic" structures.)

In the "garbage can" model of organizational cognition by Cohen, March, and Olsen (1972), it

is noted that each situation has an allied
energy level required for its solution. Each
entity in the organization (each person or
group) has a pool of energy from which to draw.
The organization ceases being aware of situations whenever they (1) have been successfully
dealt with (the problems in them have been
solved and/or the choices made) or (2) have
exhausted the energies of those coping with
them. Occasionally, in case (2), these situations are passed elsewhere in the organization, typically upward. Thus, the organization
may be viewed as a large caldron in which situations "bubble up" from below, as well as appear laterally when new ingredients are added
(from the outside) and when portions of the
stew begin interacting in unpredicted ways
(i.e., they may also have an endogenous origin). Finally, it should be recognized that the
four types have different required energy levels that range from the low (static routine) to
the high (continuing novel). Given the origin
of situations and the distribution of necessary and available energy levels, it is easily
understood why different strata in the organization cope with different types of situations.

PROPOSITION: At the upper, executive level of an
organization, there is unified, concentrated attention given to only those crises that are major, sur-
vival-threatening situations. Other situations are
treated differently depending upon which person introduces them and the manner in which they are presented.
Different persons command different degrees of respect. Some situations gain more attention because
they are presented as being the concern of a coalition
(see chapter 3).

PROPOSITION: The more an organizational unit's goal
is operational, the more likely SOPs will be evoked
to meet it; and the more nonoperational the goals,
the greater the reliance upon unprogrammed methods.
Of course, the more nonoperational a unit's goal is,
the more time that must be devoted to figuring out
just how the goal will be interpreted by upper-level
management; that is, how it will all work out in

practice. Then, too, it must be discerned how to translate that goal into action steps. This all implies the use of unprogrammed methods, whereas with an operational goal it is easier to establish an SOP to accomplish it.

PROPOSITION: In the cases of information overload or of time pressure, organizations tend to work on static routine situations first, continuing routine situations next, static novel situations third, and continuing novel situations last. Stated differently, organizations disdain the unusual, the complex, and the long term whenever a sense of stress is present. This behavior arises because of a felt need to have *some* demonstrable results, because following an SOP will lead to a safe, defensible outcome, and because novel situations are anxiety producers and familiar situations are anxiety reducers. Because of the pervasiveness of these behaviors, organizations take several steps to ensure that novel and continuing situations do get addressed: Deadlines are established, staff groups (see chapter 8) are created with the *sole* responsibility of addressing routine continuing problems (e.g., Research and Development, Management Science, Marketing Research), outside experts and consultants are employed to define and solve special problems, and special in-house task forces, teams, and committees are organized to investigate some issue.

PROPOSITION: When people in an organizational unit are bored, either because they have too little work to do or because their work does not pose a challenge to them, they seek additional intellectual stimulation. This may manifest itself in several ways—an increased propensity to form or join a clique, coalition, or cabal (see chapter 3); a tendency to embellish and prolong the situations they do encounter; and a proclivity to create new SOPs or alter existing ones and to garner support for them. The opportunity exists for creating new or altering old SOPs because of the surplus of energy and time available to detect new repetitive situations, design potential solutions for them, and collect support for the new SOPs, or modify existing SOPs (e.g., to generalize or specialize the applicability part, or to change the steps or sequencing of the action part).

SOPs Considered as Decision Procedures

The usual interpretation given to SOPs is not as problem-solving procedures but rather as decision-making devices. That is, SOPs select from among a set of possible responses in a standard, routinized manner. So standard is the procedure that it is possible in advance to predict the questions that will be asked of the situation and the sequence in which they will be posed. In short, the complete path by which the situation will be discriminated into a selected response is completely describable beforehand. In actual practice, SOPs have been observed in use in helping organizations decide how to price their products, how many supplies to order, what components to include in a newspaper ad, what stocks to include in a portfolio, and so on. To better understand this aspect of SOPs, it will be necessary to introduce more detail about the structure and use of SOPs and additional terminology about the decision-making process.

An SOP has the following structure: It has a pattern component and an action component. The pattern component allows the user to determine whether the SOP is applicable in a given situation; that is, whether certain conditions are satisfied. The action component is an interconnected series of tests and action steps; which action steps are taken depend upon the particular results of the test sequence. For example, an inventory handler's SOPs may resemble the following:

SOP 1:
Pattern: Received new information about product
          p?
   Yes → Execute action part.
    No → Try pattern part of some other SOP.

Action: End of month in < one week?
　Yes → Order 100 units.
　　No → Try next test.
　　　　Is inventory level for product p < 50
　　　　units?
　Yes → Order 500 units.
　　No → Try next test.
　　　　Is inventory level for product p > 900
　　　　units?
　Yes → Execute SOP 2.
　　No → Relax.

SOP 2
Pattern: Excessive inventory for a product?
　Yes → Execute action part.
　　No → Try pattern part of some other SOP.

Action: Contact production department; learn
　　　　a. If production rate has increased.
　　　　b. If so, whether the increase is
　　　　　　temporary or permanent.
　Temporary increase → Relax.
　Permanent increase → Notify marketing de-
　　　　　　　　　　　partment; lower param-
　　　　　　　　　　　eter values in SOP 1.
　No change in rate → Notify superior.

You can tell from this sample SOP, there are
several parameters (50 units, 500 units, 100
units, 900 units, production rate); there are
several widely different actions possible,
ranging from no action to triggering other
SOPs. The SOPs could be easily expanded to
cover more situations or contracted to be more
narrow, and since actions are differentially
selected, it is a decision-making procedure.
　SOPs are typically encoded as "discriminative nets," in which information is filtered
through a series of tests, finally resulting
in some chosen action. For example, consider
this SOP your garage may use to correct problems with an automobile's windshield washers
(the chosen actions are circled). It should be
readily apparent that discrimination nets
represent process models of SOPs considered as

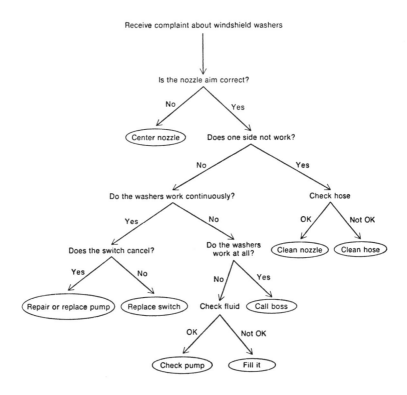

state-transition diagrams as discussed in chapter 1. The different tests are symptomatic of different *states* (of knowledge) and the results of the tests (yes/no, OK/not OK) encode *events*. Naturally, paths are encoded by the sequence of tests and results necessary to arrive at some action (e.g., to get to "Replace switch").

Decision processes involve, explicitly or implicitly, five stages (see Eilon, 1969, for example):

1. identification and formulation of the situation
2. generation of alternatives

3. formulation of an objective or an evaluation function
4. selection of best alternative
5. implementation of the chosen action.

Decision processes are usually placed into different categories depending upon the characteristics of the second, third, and fourth steps. A decision case which admits a large number of action alternatives to be generated so as to be available all at the same time *and* involves evaluation criteria which permit simultaneous mutual comparison of all alternatives is called an *optimizing decision* (see March and Simon, 1958, pp. 140-141). For example, if a number of capital investment projects are presented to a finance committee and if they employ the criterion of minimizing the outlay, then that is an optimal decision procedure. (The inventory example previously discussed could also be made into an optimizing decision. For example, consider all possible reorder quantities, and minimize the sum of warehouse costs and stockout costs.)

However, if the decision situation is so structured that it is very difficult to generate more than one alternative at a time *and* if the evaluation criteria are only threshold filters (i.e., they report only "above or not above" some crucial limit), then it is called a *satisficing decision*. For example, if it is necessary to agree upon a final design for an interplanetary spacecraft that can hold three 180-pound people for up to 21 days at a cost of $10,000,000, then each of those serves as a threshold filter—a design that holds three 190-pound people for up to 21 days at a projected cost of $9,500,000 is acceptable, whereas a design that only holds three 175-pound people for up to 24 days at a cost of $11,000,000 is unacceptable. Since it is probably very difficult to generate a number of such designs at once, this is a satisficing decision.

The five-stage decision sequence previously

exhibited is only correct, strictly speaking, for optimizing decisions. For satisficing decisions, the process must be rewritten in some form such as:

1. Identification and formulation of the situation.
2. Formulation of the threshold filters.
3. Generation of an alternative.
4. Test the alternative.
   a. accept it if it passes all threshold filters.
   b. Otherwise, go back to step 3.
5. Implementation of the chosen action.

Finally, another possible type of decision situation is called *constrained optimization*. In this instance, there are action alternatives readily available, but the only evaluation criteria are threshold filters. In the case of satisficing, the first alternative to meet or exceed all the filters would be the chosen alternative. But in the case of constrained optimization, a two-step process is followed: First, *all* the alternatives are evaluated by the filters; and second, those alternatives that pass the filters are compared against one another by constructing optimizing criteria (e.g., by constructing tradeoffs among the threshold filters—five pounds of weight equal to $100,000 in spacecraft cost). This process optimizes on a subset of the original set of alternatives.

The stages involved in the constrained optimization decision sequence are as indicated:

1. identification and formulation of the situation
2. formulation of the threshold filters
3. calculation of the tradeoffs among the evaluation criteria
4. generation of action alternatives
5. use of threshold filters to prune the set of alternatives

6. use of tradeoff functions to calculate the best remaining action alternative
7. implementation of the chosen action.

Because SOPs pre-identify the admissible set of action alternatives, they rarely represent optimizing decisions. Usually, SOPs encode a satisficing decision process. This is often due to the way in which SOPs are created--many times SOPs are little more than codifications of habit, of "the way things have always been done around here." Often there is a good rationale for part of the SOP process, but other parts of it are suboptimal, inefficient, and/or redundant. Even relying upon SOPs, it is easily possible for management to construct boundedly optimal decision processes. The first step is to uncover and record the details of what are sometimes unstated, unarticulated, and even unconscious SOPs. Then from detailed knowledge of the SOPs it is possible to construct a set of threshold filters to apply to the sequentially generated alternatives and to construct a set of tradeoff relations to evaluate those alternatives that pass the tests. But the ability to construct the constrained optimization procedures directly depends on the levels of detailed knowledge of the SOPs. An illustration of this procedure of changing a satisficing decision into a constrained optimization decision will be given later, when we consider Clarkson' (1962) study of the construction of a portfolio of common stocks.

SOPs AND ORGANIZATIONAL BEHAVIOR

There are many, many SOPs in use in an organization. One could easily, and correctly, characterize an organization as a network of SOPs, and one could account for most of the substantial distinctiveness between two organizations by carefully stating the action and

pattern parts of comparable SOPs. Since there
is such a proliferation of SOPs in organizations, it is worthwhile to consider the benefits and costs that SOPs have for organizations. For example, Cyert and March (1963, pp.
101-113) describe four major categories of SOPs
in use in organizations: to perform tasks; to
keep records and issue reports; to filter,
condense, and distribute information; and to
create and adhere to plans, schedules, and
budgets. These activities blanket virtually all
of an organization's behavior; this degree of
investment in and commitment to SOPs can only
be due to the advantages gained from them, but
there are also dysfunctional aspects of SOPs.

The many benefits from SOPs include the
stability and consistency imparted to organizational decision-making, the predictability in
behavior necessary for coordination of diverse
activities (see chapter 7), and the accumulation of knowledge and transfer of learning that
is possible by aggregating a set of SOPs. SOPs
serve as a form of organizational "memory";
they establish precedents to guide future decisions. Using SOPs reduces the need for continually engaging in active problem-solving;
recall that this requires high-energy levels
whereas only low-energy input is needed to
carry out SOPs. Also, SOPs protect people psychologically—besides requiring little energy,
the use of SOPs is always defensible. (Incidentally, it should be noted that when organizations hire new personnel, they are largely
purchasing the potential to execute SOPs and
the knowledge of a particular body of SOPs--
e.g., accountants, engineers, public relations
experts, market analysts, economists, etc. For
the organization to train someone or to send
him back to school is to try to get him to as-
similate more SOPs. For the organization to
promote someone is to communicate a belief in
his ability to learn and execute a broader
range of SOPs.) Others argue that intraorganizational conflict can be reduced by the use of
SOPs (get agreement on the rules and the

disputes will take care of themselves). Some
persons (e.g., Cyert and March, 1963) feel that
organizations disdain uncertainty in their
environments and use SOPs to cope with and
otherwise avoid uncertainty.

In spite of this impressive array of advantages, there are a number of potential dangers
when using SOPs and the dysfunctions of SOPs
can be dramatic indeed (for example, see Joseph
Heller's novel, *Catch-22*, 1961). Although SOPs
quickly focus attention, they may do so er-
roneously and cause the battle to be won but
the war to be lost. Problems of lesser importance may be attended to first (partly because
they may be easier to handle since an SOP
exists for them), and important problems may
be altogether neglected. SOPs engender "incrementalism" in the organization's cognition.
Rather than occasionally divorcing itself from
the immediate pressures to determine what is
globally optimal, the organization may adopt a
"patch-up" philosophy—attempt to fine-tune
existing SOPs or add more SOPs to correct deficiencies in the current ones when what is
really needed is a whole new approach to its
problems. Piecemeal solutions only work for so
long. One also finds SOPs created for a very
good purpose, but then they are sometimes put
to a second and perverse use. For example,
legitimate government census-taking and record-
keeping can easily slide into illegitimate sur-
veillance of citizens.

When there are massive numbers of SOPs in an
organization, as there often are, the worst
features of bureaucracy can arise, including
rigidity, nonadaptiveness, and unresponsive-
ness. As SOPs proliferate, they almost take on
an existence of their own—above, beyond, and
apart from the people in the organization.
Also, with large numbers of SOPs, it is possible for SOPs to be inappropriately executed
(e.g., "old business" being routinely attended
to in the midst of a crisis). It is also possible to develop inconsistencies between different SOPs, as the same situation is

attacked by different parts of the organization.

Given the weight, pervasiveness, and perversity of these potential problems with SOPs, wise managers concern themselves with the issues of when (and how) to design an original SOP, to terminate using an SOP, and to change and redesign an SOP.

DESIGNING AND ALTERING SOPs

Probably one of the most troublesome issues facing middle and top management is the creation, monitoring, and changing of appropriate and adequate SOPs. There are essentially five design issues in the creation of a new SOP:

1. Identification of a repetitively occurring situation.
2. Knowledge of all the relevant variables.
3. Development of a set of action rules.
4. Factorization of the situation-action rule linkages into unit SOPs such that:
   a. a unit SOP can be readily learned and executed by a person or organizational team.
   b. there is unity and wholeness to the SOP (rather than being a fractionated part).
   c. interdependence with other SOPs is minimized.
   d. any coordination requirements are built into the SOP.
5. Dissemination of information about the new SOPs and training in their use.

To consider these issues in more detail, consider the following example. Consider a young, growing organization that for the first time experiences a turnover—an employee quits for what he feels is a better job. In the example organization, a number of alternative responses to this problem are possible:

• Ignore the turnover and everyone continue doing what he did before.

- Try to learn if other employees are dissatisfied and are ready to quit.
- Redesign the organization so the activities of the person who quit are incorporated in other people's roles.
- Attempt to recruit someone to fill the vacancy.
- See if anyone currently employed is qualified and willing to fill the vacancy.

All of the responses listed for the problem essentially treat it as a one-shot affair: solve it and this worry is over. What is needed is someone who can recognize that this is (or will be) a repetitive problem—people will continue to leave the organization for a variety of reasons. This insight has come from either an analysis of historical data, an analysis of comparable organizations, or a projection of future trends. The person making this assessment looks for patterns in his records, in human behavior, and in the events that occur around him.

After having identified the repetitively occurring situation, the hypothetical manager has to define the situation as broadly as he can. The factors and variables he uncovers will be used in the later stages of the design process. The situation may involve turnover due to resignation, retirement, transfer, promotion, death, or disability. The turnover may be in any department or division in the company, and it may involve a worker from any level.

The action rules are essentially the responses that the organization would like to make to the problem. Suppose the company considers the following as reasonable possible responses to the turnover problem:

- Conduct exit interviews to determine the reason for leaving.
- Announce the position vacancy within the firm.
- Advertise the vacancy outside of the firm.
- Interview at least three candidates.
- Select the best qualified person.

These are rather broad, but they will be re-
fined into more detailed steps as the unit
SOPs are developed.

In developing unit SOPs, the designer will
probably wish to partition the situation into
mutually exclusive classes. For example, he
may construct the six classes:

• voluntary blue-collar turnover
• involuntary blue-collar turnover
• voluntary white-collar turnover
• involuntary white-collar turnover
• voluntary executive-level turnover
• involuntary executive-level turnover

Among the reasons for constructing these classes is that the desired organizational responses (the SOPs) will be slightly different
in all six classes. For voluntary blue-collar
turnover it probably suffices to learn why the
person is quitting, to advertise the position,
and to hire the first applicant who meets or
exceeds the skill requirements. However, for
involuntary executive-level turnover, the organization would probably prefer to replace
only from within and to conduct extensive in-
terviewing to ensure the selected person will
mesh properly with the rest of the management
team.

Thus, the SOPs developed will have to test
to see which subsituation is present and then
take differential actions. Different SOPs will
probably be handled by different people (e.g.,
junior members of the personnel department for
blue-collar turnover and more senior members
for white-collar). Any interdependencies will
have to be built into the SOPs (e.g., contact-
ing union representatives in the case of blue-
collar turnover, working with an advertising
department in the case of executive-level turnover).

An organization's troubles do not cease with
the creation of SOPs that appear adequate and
appropriate to cope with a particular situation. There remain problems of:

1. communication
2. acceptance
3. training
4. misapplication
5. control
6. adaptation.

The communication problems consist of informing people about the new SOP, so they can either use it, plan on its being used, or understand the need for the codification of the behavior. How is the communication to be handled—a memo? A meeting? Publication in a newsletter? Let word leak out through the informal network? Kiesler (1978) addresses some of the issues concerning types of communication processes and their effectiveness in different cases.

Although effective communication is necessary to inform people of the new SOP and the reason for its existence, this is no guarantee that people will accept the SOP or the rationale behind it. Numerous persuasion techniques may be needed to get acceptance of the SOP. Examples of such methods are: attempts to force attitude consistency (see Jabes, 1978)—to admire the company you must also accept its rules; influence and conformity pressure (see Kiesler, 1978)—if most people in a work group accept the SOP, probably all the members will; and leadership and power (see Simmons, 1978)—the leaders have the perspective and set an example for the others to follow.

Training refers to the problems encountered in assigning SOPs to people and in instructing them in how to use their SOPs and how to plan on the use of SOPs by others, that is, to coordinate their behaviors (see Simmons, 1978, ch. 5).

Misapplication of SOPs occurs whenever an SOP is applied to some situation it *should not* have been applied to, whenever it is not applied to a situation it *should* have been applied to, and whenever two or more SOPs compete for

application to a situation. The most usual
cases of organizational misapplication of SOPs
are the first and the third. As an example of
the first case, consider the slavish personnel
worker who doggedly applies his turnover SOP
when 15 of 18 blue-collar workers in one production unit quit the job. This is no occasion
to be seeking 15 new workers; this is a sign
of a need for some problem-solving. As an example of the second case, consider a salesman
who is hired away from a subsidiary by the
parent firm to work as a foreman. Two more SOPs
may be evoked since it is not clear whether

- This is a promotion, a transfer, or a resignation.
- The worker is blue-collar or white-collar.

Either case of misapplication is a clear sign
for the need to redesign the SOPs, that is, to
go through the previously discussed five-stage
design process afresh.

The control problems with SOPs are the difficulties in learning whether misapplication of
them is occurring and whether they are being
executed properly. Word will eventually reach
management of wholesale resignations or of
power struggles between two or more units
fighting for jurisdiction, but if this information is slow in reaching management, or if
management does not seek out data on how well
the execution of SOPs is being conducted, this
is not a healthy sign for the organization.
For example, the quality of SOP execution is
very important for those people occupying organizational "boundary" roles—those people who
come into frequent contact with persons outside
of the organization (customers, suppliers,
salesmen, newsmen, governmental representatives, etc.). Lackadaisical execution or misapplication of SOPs can have serious effects
upon the organization's viability.

Finally, times and circumstances change, and
SOPs must change, too. Two types of changes in
SOPs are worth exploring: change in degree and
change in kind. Changes in degree are merely

parametric variations on the same old SOPs,
for example, instead of reordering 25 units,
reorder 35; instead of hiring a person with 2
years of college, seek a B.A. or B.S. degree;
instead of the markup being 40%, make it 50%;
instead of issuing a report every quarter, issue monthly reports. Changes in parameter values are easily assimilated into SOPs and are
easily accepted by the people in the organization. Luckily, this type of change is more frequent than the second type. However, recogniz-
ing the need for the change is not so readily
accomplished.

Changes in kind mean that a new SOP is being
instituted; either a major modification is
being made to an existing SOP or a brand new
SOP is being installed where discretion was
relied upon previously. In either event, the
previously discussed misapplication and control
problems emerge again, along with a new one:
resistance to change (see Pfeffer, 1978).

Besides resistance to the change, and, naturally, the design of a new (or redesign of an
old) SOP, the biggest difficulty in introducing
a change in kind lies in identifying the need
for the change. To what signals does one react?
How long does one patch up existing SOPs? How
does one decide that a new SOP is needed for a
situation or that an existing SOP is either inadequate or inappropriate? These are not facile
questions for which a ready answer can be supplied. Rather, these represent open questions
that will be researched as the field of organizational science matures.

For example, some of the variables that *may*
have an effect on whether or not an SOP is
changed and whether the change is in degree or
in kind are (1) the energy levels required and
available for those activities; (2) the types
of search procedures (see chapter 6) needed
and evoked for the changes; (3) the number of
difficulties resulting from the application of
the SOP; (4) and the importance of the problems
stemming from the use of the SOP. It is easy to
tie some of these variables into propositions;

it is less clear what the actual process is
that people use in deciding when and how to
change SOPs.

PROPOSITION: SOPs are not changed when their application results in few, mostly unimportant problems, and
when the effort needed to effect a change is enormous.

PROPOSITION: An SOP is changed in degree when its use
results in many minor problems, when there is sufficient energy available to cause the change, and
when little searching is required to decide on what
the change should be.

PROPOSITION: An SOP is changed in kind when it pro-
duces many major problems, where there is sufficient
time and energy to design a new one and get acceptance of it, and when a search procedure exists for
successfully redesigning the SOP.

EXAMPLES OF SOPS

Five examples of SOPs used in organizations
are next sketched; ample reference is supplied
for those five cases and for others that are
merely alluded to so that full detail can be
found. These five cases were selected because
they represent actual contemporary descriptions
of organizational behavior and because they illustrate the diversity and perversity of SOP
use within and across organizations of different types.

G.P.E. Clarkson (1962) has discovered that
the development of a portfolio of common stocks
for a trust by a bank's officer is conducted
through an SOP, a satisficing SOP contrary to
the usual maximizing procedures advocated by
financial theorists such as Markowitz (1959).
Actually, there are several different SOPs executed depending upon whether the goal of the
account is primarily growth, income, or some
combination. The process is triggered by a
client arriving at the trust investor's office
to announce that he desires a trust to be set
up in the amount of x dollars. There then ensues a discussion of the client's wishes and

his current socioeconomic state. After the goal
of the account has been ascertained, the trust
investment officer applies one of several SOPs
which (1) select which industries will be rep-
resented in the portfolio; (2) select the
stocks to be purchased from those industries;
and (3) select the number of shares of each
stock to be purchased.

The actual stock selection process revealed
by Clarkson is rather interesting, since it
represents a case in which management, were
they to uncover the SOP, could modify the decision process from being one of satisficing to
being one of constrained optimization. The process used was to scan sequentially the industries in alphabetical order (e.g., Airlines,
Automobiles, Banks, Building, Container, . . .)
and to sequentially scan the stocks within that
industry in alphabetical order (e.g., American
Airlines, Continental Airlines, Delta Airlines,
Eastern Airlines, . . .). The first stock that
met or exceeded all of the threshold tests was
accepted for inclusion in the portfolio, and
the scanner then skipped to the next alphabetical industry. Of course, one way to convert
this to a bounded optimization process would
be to apply the SOP to *all* stocks in an industry, and then apply some mutual comparison
(weighted sums of the threshold filters?) to
all stocks accepted by the SOP.

Clarkson's understanding of these processes
is so complete that he was able to construct a
computer program whose behavior was virtually
indistinguishable from that of the human trust
investment officer. This is primarily due to
his ability to record the SOPs as discrimination nets. Not only can he represent the procedure by which an investment policy is selected as a discrimination net (see Clarkson, 1962,
p. 47), but he can also so represent the processes by which a stock is included or rejected
in the portfolio (pp. 110-111) and of how many
shares of chosen stock will be purchased (p.
112). As but *one* example of the detail in SOPs
he has uncovered, consider the following

slightly simplified discrimination net for
including or rejecting common stocks in a trust
fund, when the goal of the account is primarily
capital appreciation (again, the chosen actions
are circled):

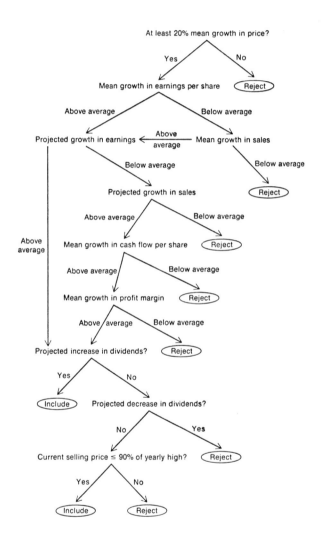

Clarkson's work is important not only for the unusual SOP he uncovered but also because of the important financial decision-making that he showed was occurring in this for-profit firm. J. P. Crecine (1967) and D. Gerwin (1969) have studied other financial decisions made through SOPs in public, not-for-profit organizations: the budgeting process in municipal governments (Crecine) and school boards (Gerwin). The budgeting process appears to be triggered by a single event: the right "time." When "budget time" is present, a solicitation for expenditure requests is made. (Note that this SOP triggers other SOPs—the process used by department heads to estimate expenditure levels for the next fiscal year. Sometimes, games are played: "I need 10% more than this year's budget, so I'll request 20% and expect to be argued down to what I really want.") While waiting for the expenditure requests to come in, revenue estimates are made. Only when projected revenues and expenditure requests are grossly different is problem-solving initiated. There are SOPs to handle the normal cases when they are not exactly equal, but approximate one another.

The budgeting example shows how SOPs may be interdependent, how they may trigger one another, and how they may evoke problem-solving as well. Although private, for-profit firms are more secretive about their budgeting processes, those processes are presumably not too different from the ones revealed by Crecine and Gerwin.

Lest anyone feel that SOPs per se represent the height of organizational rationality, A. I. Solzhenitsyn (1973) has pictured a world of SOPs gone mad. The "pattern" part of SOPs used by the state police in the U.S.S.R. is so vague and ambiguous as to admit practically *any* behavior. (For example, Section 6 of Article 58: Contacts Leading to Suspicion of Espionage: " . . . an acquaintance of an acquaintance of your wife had a dress made by the same seamstress . . . used by the wife of a foreign diplomat" [p. 64]; and again, Section 1, Article 58: " . . . any action [and, . . . any absence of action] directed toward the weakening of state power was considered to be counterrevolutionary" [pp. 60-61].) Also, the state police, in applying these vague "patterns", arrest friends, relatives, neighbors, and acquaintances of those arrested, and in some instances even arrest those standing or walking *near* the individual who is being arrested. As the quotas (of arrested persons) assigned to the state police change, the pattern part of these SOPs is interpreted and applied rather more broadly or narrowly as needed. These SOPs, rather than permitting stability and predictability, lead to *greater* uncertainty and anxiety. Solzhenitsyn also reports that there are few, mostly ineffectual, SOPs for releasing "innocent" people once arrested. To be arrested is to be convicted.

R. M. Cyert and J. G. March (1963) supply the fourth and fifth examples of SOP use. In the study of the behavior in a large metropolitan department store, they found that the procedure used to set prices on merchandise was governed by SOPs. When an item arrived to be priced and sold, a price was set by applying a predetermined markup rate to its cost and setting the selling price to be the item's cost plus its markup. When a sale (e.g., a white sale or a clearance sale) or a markdown occurred (items that did not move quickly were marked down), other pricing SOPs were followed.

Cyert and March also studied the inventory procedures and the sales forecasting of the department. Again, they found that SOPs were used to determine how much of some item to order (a fraction of the seasonal sales estimate—which is a function of last year's sales) and how much to reorder when the item is "nearly" sold out (a function of the currently available stock, the minimum stock desired, and the recent sales history).

Examples four and five illustrate that the crucial economic decisions of profit-oriented firms (How large a quantity of some goods should we supply to the marketplace? What should we price it at?) are made by SOPs. Examples two and three demonstrate that SOPs are also employed by other types of firms for some of their quasi-economic (budgeting) and non-economic (pragmatic application of the law) decision behaviors.

SOPs used in different organizational types for a variety of problems have been studied by other researchers. To exhibit some of the diversity and to provide a pointer to some of the research literature, a *very* brief description of some of these studies will be provided. D. Rados (1972) found the SOPs used to compose advertising copy. C. E. Weber (1965, p. B70) unraveled the SOPs used in determining " . . . the size and composition of the staff of an electronic data processing department in a company." J. A. Howard and W. M. Morgenroth (1968) were able to describe the SOP used by a high company executive making a major pricing decision. O. A. Davis and F. H. Rueter (1972) detailed the SOPs used by a municipal government in making zoning decisions. Finally, in the book edited by C. E. Weber and G. Peters (1969), there appeared several articles describing a number of different SOPs in use for such decisions as industrial purchasing, vendor selection, and interlibrary loans.

REFERENCES

Clarkson, G.P.E. *Portfolio Selection: A Simulation of Trust Investment.* Englewood Cliffs, N.J.: Prentice-Hall, 1962.

Cohen, M. D., March, J. G., and Olsen, J. P. " A Garbage Can Model of Organizational Choice." *Administrative Science Quarterly* 17, no. 1 (March 1972): 1-25.

Crecine, J. P. "A Computer Simulation Model of Municipal Budgeting." *Management Science* 13, no. 11 (July 1967): 786-815.

Cyert, R. M., and March, J. G. *A Behavioral Theory of the Firm.* Englewood Cliffs, N.J.: Prentice-Hall, 1963.

Davis, O. A., and Rueter, F. H. "A Simulation of Municipal Zoning Decisions." *Management Science* 19, no. 4 (December 1972): P-39 to P-77.

Eilon, S. "What Is a Decision?" *Management Science* 16, no. 4 (December 1969): B-172 to B-189.

Gerwin, D. "A Process Model of Budgeting in a Public School System." *Management Science* 15, no. 7 (March 1969): 338-361.

Heller, J. *Catch-22.* New York: Simon and Shuster, 1961.

Howard, J. A., and Morgenroth, W. M. "Information-Processing Model of Executive Decision." *Management Science* 14, no. 7 (March 1968): 416-428.

Jabes, J. *Individual Processes in Organizational Behavior.* Arlington Heights, Ill.: AHM Publishing Corporation, 1978.

Kiesler, S. *Interpersonal Processes in Groups and Organizations.* Arlington Heights, Ill.: AHM Publishing Corporation, 1978.

March, J. G., and Simon, H. A. *Organizations.* New York: Wiley, 1958.

Markowitz, H. *Portfolio Selection: Efficient Diversification of Investments.* New York: Wiley, 1959.

Pfeffer, J. *Organizational Design.* Arlington Heights, Ill.: AHM Publishing Corporation, 1978.

Rados, D. L. "Selection and Evaluation of Alternatives in Repetitive Decision-Making." *Administrative Science Quarterly* 17, no. 2 (June 1972): 196-206.

Simmons, R. E. *Managing Behavioral Processes: Applications of Theory and Research.* Arlington Heights, Ill.: AHM Publishing Corporation, 1978.

Simon, H. A. *Models of Man.* New York: Wiley, 1957.

Solzhenitsyn, A. I. *The Gulag Archipelago.* New York: Harper and Row, 1973.

Thompson, J. D., and Tuden, A. "Strategies, Structures and Processes of Organizational Decision." In

Comparative Studies in Administration, edited by J. D. Thompson, et al. Pittsburgh, Penn.: University of Pittsburgh Press, 1959.

Weber, C. E. "Intraorganizational Decision Processes Influencing the EDP Staff Budget." *Management Science* 12, no. 4 (December 1965): B69–B93.

Weber, C. E., and Peters, G. *Management Action: Models of Administrative Decisions*. Scranton, Penn.: International Textbook, 1969.

5

Management by Objectives

Management by objectives (usually referred to by its acronym, MBO), is a broadly painted procedure (i.e., details have to be worked out in each organization that uses it), almost a philosophy of management, for improving aspects of an organization's performance such as higher productivity, greater commitment, reduced turnover, and so on. It systematizes a method of setting differential goals for each person in the organization. Since each person's objectives are practically "tailor-made," so the argument goes, each person will work harder and be more involved in the job, and the desired benefits will ensue. Observe that this proposition is normative, or prescriptive in nature; *all* of the other chapters in this book concern descriptions, not prescriptions, of organizational behavior. This exception is made because the MBO technique is a continually

ongoing process, whereas other so-called normative guidelines for organizations are not. For
example, they usually involve setting a variable to one state or another—the leader is to
be directive or permissive; the span of control is to be 5, 6, 7, 8, or 9; the communication network is to be all-channel, circle, or
wheel.

The concept of management by objectives was
first introduced by Drucker (1954). As the
name of his book suggests, MBO originated in
managerial practice and was later codified,
systematized, empirically studied, and publi-
cized by academic researchers such as McGregor
(1960). In one sense, MBO is an extension of
the theory of participative management. The
theory argues that by allowing subordinates to
have a voice in decision-making (through a
variety of devices), productivity will be
higher, costs will be lower, better decisions
will result, decisions will be more readily
accepted, people will be more satisfied with
their jobs, and so on. Likert (1961), in two
case studies, reports that participative management allowed some of those benefits to be
realized; however, Morse and Reimer (1956) note
no significant favorable change from using
participative management.

Other ways of viewing MBO in an historical
manner are that it is an outcropping of the job
enlargement/job enrichment literatures, but
they too have an uneven success rate (e.g.,
Hulin and Blood, 1968, note that the success
of such programs often depends upon contextual
variables). One can also view MBO as a very
sophisticated performance appraisal system; a
clever method for assessing a person's contributions to the organization by first getting
him to agree to an operational set of short-
term goals. It is true that there are many
complexities to a good performance appraisal
system (see Ridgway, 1956, for some of the
problems involved in devising an adequate system) and that MBO overcomes many of those

difficulties, but MBO is more than a performance appraisal system, a job enrichment device, a technique of participative management,
or a combination of them all. MBO will be
shown to be a management process.

To explicate the MBO method, I shall first
differentiate MBO from other management practices, then examine the claimed advantages and
philosophy of MBO, and finally construct a
theory consistent with MBO. Practical experience with MBO is related by investigating the
preconditions necessary for it, by reporting
the problems of implementation which have aris-
en, and by recounting the individual experiences of firms that have put MBO into practice.

THE METHOD AND PHILOSOPHY OF MBO

Management by objectives is a system in
which immediate superior-subordinate pairs
throughout the organization periodically meet
to discuss three things: (1) what the subordinate should try to accomplish during the next
time period, in the most operational terms
practicable; (2) what actions or methods the
subordinate might reasonably use in order to
accomplish his goals; (3) how well the subordinate accomplished the goals set at the start
of the last time period, noting the exogenous
factors (e.g., personal illness, labor strike,
recent transfer to this job) that may have affected the subordinate's performance. MBO is a
process for planning work and reviewing its
degree of accomplishment. It is crucial to
note that the three steps repeat themselves,
say, every three months, so it is important to
amplify upon these steps.

Realistically, MBO is usually aimed at getting higher levels of performance from lower-
level employees who usually produce output of
a standardized quality. But MBO is more than a
trick or a gimmick, because in return for
higher levels of performance, MBO trades fair

and just performance evaluations and a certain degree of control over goal-setting and activity patterns.

Regarding the goal-setting activity, the following is a typical sequence: First, the superior announces what he would like the subordinate to accomplish during the time period; the subordinate then makes a counter-offer; and finally the pair of them negotiates or bargains until a mutually agreeable set of goals for the subordinate is found. It is crucial that (1) the goals be mutually agreed upon, (2) the goals be as operational as possible, and (3) the power differential between superior and subordinate be kept in the background. Other scenarios that frequently occur are for the superior to accept whatever goals the subordinate announces, for a premeeting to occur in which both parties exchange views but have sufficient time to reflect upon the premeeting before the actual goal-setting meeting takes place, and for goal planning to occur in one set of meetings and performance review to be conducted separately.

Regarding the accomplishment of goals, they must appear feasible to the subordinate, he must know the relevant techniques to accomplish them, and he must be sufficiently competent with those techniques. It is the superior's duty to see that the subordinate has had the proper education, training, and experiences so that it is possible to expect a diligent effort to succeed.

Regarding the work review activity, it should be noted that individuals are *not* to be evaluated on the basis of relatively nonoperational criteria (such as "honesty" or "initiative"), but rather using the verifiable, job-related criteria developed in phase (1) of the previous time period (see Odiorne, 1965).

To better understand what MBO is, and is not, it is useful to contrast it to two similar-sounding concepts with which it is sometimes mistakenly confused: (1) the use of goals, and

(2) management by exception. MBO is not merely the use of goals; all organizations use goals (as discussed in chapter 2). However, in many organizations statements about goals originate at the top and are often largely nonoperational. As they filter down through the organization the goals acquire nuances, biases, and characteristics of the managers who supply operational meaning to them. The use of goals allows people to be controlled; MBO shifts the aim to the control of task processes. MBO stresses operationality of goals (at all levels) and stresses the agreeability of the goals to each superior-subordinate pair (rather than the superior declaring to the subordinate what his goals are to be). Furthermore, since a record is made of the agreed-upon goals (for the review phase occurring at the end of the period), the superior's own superiors can check up on him (and they usually do) to see what the goals are of the people in their unit. This has the effect of ensuring greater consistency in goals up and down all levels of the organization.

Management by exception is the philosophy or principle in which management sets standards of performance for units and individuals throughout an organization. Then, whenever actual performance significantly varies in an unfavorable direction from the established standard, that aspect of the organization is scrutinized to learn why the exception occurred, to correct it, and if at all possible, to prevent it from ever happening again. In the use of MBO, one attends not only exceptionally poor performance, but also exceptionally good performance as well as the usual case of standard performance. Furthermore, accountability is obvious under MBO, which is not so under management by exception.

Of course, MBO is easily differentiated from standard performance appraisal systems by its insistence upon operational, job-related criteria integrated into the organizational goal system. It is also clearly different from

ordinary techniques of participative management due to the inclusion of, and emphasis
upon, performance review and appraisal.

An organization that employs MBO can expect
to enjoy many advantages, according to propo-
nents of MBO (Drucker, 1954; Odiorne, 1965;
Carroll and Tosi, 1973; Raia, 1974). Missions,
objectives, and responsibilities are supposed
to be clarified because of the stress on oper-
ationalism in the goals. Involving subordinates
in the goal-setting process is supposed to increase their motivation, improve their attitudes toward the work setting, and because of
their commitment to the goals they have helped
produce, their productivity is claimed to be
greater. MBO emphasizes self-determination and
self-motivation of the employee. For a variety
of reasons, MBO is supposed to lead to improved
personal growth and development of potential:
subordinate involvement in the process, the
short-term focus on operational, attainable
goals, keying the performance appraisal to the
agreed-upon goals, and so on. A central theme
is that adopting MBO will lead to improved
planning and organization of work. (If a unit
is supposed to attempt some task, the manager
of that unit must find at least one subordinate
willing to accept responsibility for that task;
hence better, more conscientious planning and
division of labor by the manager of that unit.)
Pounds (1969) reports that many managers spend
much time working on other people's problems.
Assuming that the managers are all basically
competent, and they usually are, then another
benefit of MBO is that it forces people to focus upon their own work. Additional benefits
could be discussed, but the ones illustrated
should give some depth to the advantages claimed
to be gained by using MBO. The empirical validity of some of those claims will be reported
later when case studies of organizations which
have used MBO are related. However, all the
benefits of MBO can be negated by failing to
satisfy any one of the five necessary preconditions (also discussed in the next section).

The final two points in the philosophy of
MBO relate to the discussions of organizational goals (in chapter 2) and of organizational
effectiveness (in chapter 9). MBO is one device for elaborating and stabilizing organizational goals. The elaboration occurs as top-
level superiors negotiate their goals with
their supervisors and then interact with their
subordinates to produce their goals, as the
subordinates then bargain with those immediately beneath them. The stabilization occurs
in two ways. First, the goals are in effect
for at least the duration of the time period,
which is often three months and sometimes six
months in length. Of course, the same goals
can also be in effect for multiple time periods. The second way that MBO stabilizes goals
is due to its remarkable property of being most
useful and most successful in nonrecurring
situations. That is, consider an organization
that is faced with stable, routine, and recurring problems, decisions, and situations,
such as a clerical organization or a factory
producing a common amount of a standard product using a constant technology. In such cases, management is responsible for setting performance standards and enforcing adherence to these standards. If
MBO were applied in such cases, there would be
little to negotiate after goals had been set
the first few periods. The usefulness, and
eventual success, of MBO would be greatly reduced in such cases. The costs of installing
and maintaining an MBO system overwhelm the
benefits which can be expected from MBO in
those situations. (In these repetitive cases,
the proper thing for management to do is to
design and implement standard operating procedures; see chapter 4.) Instead, MBO works
best when there are modest environmental fluctuations, novel problems, unusual circumstances, and nonrecurring situations. In those
cases, negotiation can proceed with zest, and
once the goals filter down through the organization and are agreed upon, the organization's
goals are effectively stabilized.

It should also be recognized that management
by objectives is an example of techniques for
improving organizational processes; that is,
MBO is one of a very few methods that has demonstrated consistent success at increasing organizational effectiveness. (Tersely, and
crudely, organizational efficiency refers to
the use made of inputs, usually measured by
the ratio of output to input; however, organizational effectiveness refers to how well the
organization achieves its goals, usually measured by the rate of return of resources to
the system (see chapter 9). Because MBO is a
procedure that involves everyone in the organization in the formation of its goals, because
the goals are operational, and because people's
performances are evaluated against their own
goals, the achievement of the overall organizational goals is facilitated. Furthermore,
because of the performance review and performance evaluation systems incorporated in MBO,
the achievement level of each individual's
goals, as well as, cumulatively, overall organizational goals, is enhanced. Thus, employing MBO tends to improve organizational effectiveness.

THE THEORY BEHIND MBO

Frankly, the literature of MBO does not supply its own theoretical justification. Instead,
MBO is usually written up as a "successful
method" or a "new philosophy for management"
or "an effective change technique" or some such
title (for other procedures for changing organizational behavior that also lack theoretical underpinnings, see Pfeffer, 1978). To
rectify this situation, I will sketch a tentative allusion to theoretical support for MBO.
The path-goal theory of leader effectiveness
by House (1971) supplies the reasoning for the
success of the superior-subordinate dyadic
negotiation and the use of operational goals.
House's path-goal theory argues that motivation

to work is a function of several factors, three of which are; (1) the extrinsic rewards associated with work accomplishment (the organizationally endowed rewards for effective behavior); (2) the intrinsic rewards of that work (the satisfaction with or pleasure in the work); and (3) the apparent linkage between work achievement and organizational rewards (the degree of belief that following a particular path—behavior—will lead to a desired outcome). The MBO procedure serves to increase the salience of the second and third variables, which means that under MBO, as claimed, people are more motivated. The intrinsic rewards are increased under MBO because the subordinate has a say in which tasks (goals) he will attempt and how he is to work at accomplishing those tasks. Also under MBO, the path instrumentality is increased if the individual believes the basis for the receipt of organizational rewards is the degree of accomplishment of the clear, objective, operational goals.

The process conception accounts for the remainder of the effectiveness of the MBO technique. MBO puts the supervisor into intimate contact with the task processes in his unit: He is made more aware of them, and he is more easily able to modify them. Thus the effectiveness of his unit is enhanced. Finally, because of the requirement of periodic review, different goals and task processes *can* be introduced at different time periods, rather than dogmatically persisting with the same set of goals and processes. Because MBO is utilized throughout the organization, it is objectively "fair," and for reasons argued previously, it should make the entire organization more effective.

One way to visualize the use of the MBO technique is through the use of state transition diagrams as discussed in chapter 1; this analysis should also convince any who are still skeptical that MBO is indeed a process technique rather than an S-R tool. Consider one superior-subordinate dyad at time t_0 in which

the outcome of the subordinate's past activities E_0 is described by state S_0; the history
of the performance of this subordinate is also
included in order to be complete.

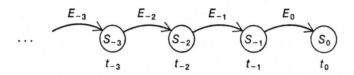

The problems now confronting the pair for them
to characterize the next state, S_1, that the
subordinate should achieve and to decide upon
the activities, E_1, that will transform S_0 into
S_1. Both decisions are contingent upon the current state and the history of performance up
to the present. Since these decisions will recur at the end of the next time period, what
we have is a state transition diagram that extends indefinitely to the right over time; that
is, we are dealing with a process. Since the
MBO procedure tracks and controls a process, it
too must be a process.

THE IMPLEMENTATION OF MBO

In order to utilize MBO, it is necessary to
establish five conditions in the organization
under consideration. Failure to institute even
one of them is sufficient to nullify the gains
that may be expected from MBO. First, there
must be total organizational commitment to MBO.
The organization must not view MBO as a short-
term experiment to be tried and possibly later
discarded. Instead, it must be made clear to
all members of the organization that henceforth
MBO will be a standard practice. Besides at-
titudinal commitment, there must also be financial and budgetary commitment (e.g., to train
people in the use of MBO), manpower commitment
(MBO is typically introduced by people in the
personnel department), and patience. Without

organizational commitment, some people will
resist the change to MBO, will fight it, and
will eventually cause the system to erode from
within.

Second, MBO must be universally applied inside the organization. Not to do so would create feelings of inequity; those excluded from
MBO wondering what is so special about those
included and those included wondering why they
are the guinea pigs. These suspicions can easily be fanned into discontent sufficient to
undermine the MBO program. However, saying that
MBO must be universally applied is not to deny
two important restraints in its application.
One, it need not be applied at all levels in
the organization; specifically, the upper echelons are exempt. For instance, there is no
single person for the president to negotiate
his goals with. More importantly, the people
at the higher levels in an organization typically deal with more nonoperational goals and
typically have longer time horizons such that
MBO is not really appropriate. Of course, it is
important that *some* layer in the organization
make the transition from nonoperational into
more operational goals. Two, MBO need not be
applied in all groups in the organization. For
example, consider the plight of a group of research scientists; how could one reasonably expect them, individually, to come up with novel
ideas on a fixed timetable? In general, MBO is
not as beneficial for those people who occupy
any type of staff role (be sure to see chapter
8 on the concept of staff); MBO will succeed
with salesmen, not with market analysts. But
with these two restraints employed in a fair
and reasonable manner, it remains the case that
MBO must be universally applied elsewhere in
the organization.

Third, for each superior-subordinate dyad,
there must be periodic goal negotiation and
performance review. The usual time periods are
monthly, quarterly, and semiannually. More frequent meetings involve too much overhead and
too short-term a focus; less frequent meetings

reduce the subordinate's sense of involvement
and minimize many of the gains to be realized
from MBO. It is inconceivable that an MBO program could possibly succeed without periodic
goal negotiation and periodic performance review. One thing that happens in using MBO is
that the dyadic negotiations become increasing-
ly more constrained (1) the farther down the
hierarchy one looks (because the higher-level
clear, operational objective has been increas-
ingly factored into more and more minute detail) and (2) the more that intraunit negotiations have progressed (if there are ten people
in a unit and the superior has agreed to goals
for nine of them, then the tenth person has to
pick up the difference between what the superior promised his boss his unit would do and
the performance goals of the first nine). An
item that does not receive much attention in
the MBO literature is, what happens when a superior-subordinate dyad fail to agree upon a
set of goals? Does negotiation continue until
consensus is reached? Does MBO break down? Is
mediation attempted? What happens when two
people, each behaving in good faith, disagree—
as occasionally will happen? Finally, during
the goal negotiation process, Levinson (1970)
points out that the organizational objective
proposed by the superior should take into account the individual subordinate's personal
objectives.

Fourth, the agreement in goals that is
reached must be as specific and as operational
as possible. If the agreed-upon goals are not
particularly operational, it becomes difficult
to conduct an honest performance appraisal at
the end of the time period. Regardless of the
outcome of such a performance review, it is
possible for both parties to feel exploited by
one another. Furthermore, the more specific the
agreement is, the higher the quality of the
direction supplied to the subordinate and the
higher the quality of his resultant performance. Varney (1972) argues that providing
clear, operational objectives is more important

to the success of an MBO program than employee
participation in the goal-setting process.
But, if one considers a job that can only be
characterized through ill-defined and vague
criteria (e.g., the "smoothness" with which
customer complaints are handled or the "quality" of nursing care that patients receive),
then to force clear, operational objectives is
probably to vulgarize the job (e.g., number of
complaints handled per day, number of refer-
rals to the boss, average length of hospital
stay per patient, average bed occupancy rate).
MBO should probably not be used with such
jobs.

Fifth, it is critical that the subordinate
know of and understand feasible actions steps
and that he be capable, skilled, and competent
enough to carry them out. It does no good for
specific goals to be periodically negotiated
if the person with those goals finds them
frustrating because he does not know how to
achieve them or because they are impossible.
This can occur more frequently than one might
first believe; recall that MBO is best employed in novel, complex, and problematic environments. When the subordinate perceives difficulty in accomplishing his goals, he should
inform his superior during the goal negotiation
interview. Then the superior has the proper
managerial responsibility of coaching, teaching, or training the subordinate so he can accomplish the goals. (In some cases, the goals
may have been patently impossible; revision of
the goals is then the only realistic way out.)

Even with these five conditions established,
there can be many problems in implementing MBO.
(Another type of problem arises when an organization ignores establishing the conditions and
goes forward in applying MBO. This often occurs because some people worship any new technique that looks promising. Similar problems
arise in attempting to use MBO in an off-the-
shelf manner, that is, with little thought
about adapting it to the peculiarities of the
organization.) I will discuss some of these

problems to show how MBO must be fine-tuned to
fit each particular organization and the diversity of factors to which management must be
sensitive and willing to react.

When MBO is being implemented, there may be
the common mistrust and suspicion that ac-
companies many major organizational changes.
Upper management, to combat those sentiments,
will have to be candid about what MBO is and
isn't and why it is being introduced in the
first place. Management will have to work hard
to assure people that it is not a trick or gimmick to squeeze more work out of them for no
increase in rewards. Relating the experiences
and attitudes of other organizations which
changed to MBO may ease some anxiety.

Top-level management is also going to have
to guard against having unattainable expectations concerning the results MBO will produce.
MBO will not rescue firms from bankruptcy, reverse falling market shares, dramatically increase earnings, or change apathy to enthusi-
asm. MBO is a procedure that apparently leads
to small, but nonnegligible, consistent improvements in an organization's performance.

Higher management also has to be cautioned
against looking for improvements in performance
quickly. It takes time for MBO to be assimilated as a standard practice. Carroll and Tosi
(1973) recommend that between three and five
years may be needed before the benefits from
MBO may start showing themselves. Ivancevich
(1974) rarely found any improvement before
eighteen months had elapsed.

Another upper management problem is the
failure to establish properly the five necessary preconditions which were elaborated earlier.

The one situation for which it is known that
MBO will not succeed is in the presence of
major organizational instability. People would
rather devote their energies to understanding
and coping with major, system-wide problems
rather than attending to the relatively short-
run, narrow goals produced by an MBO program.

The line dividing major instability (for which MBO is not good) from nonrecurring situations (which MBO is designed for) is fuzzy and hard to draw accurately. Organizational instability characteristically involves a threat to the organization's existence or involves a system-wide change to the organization. Examples of such instability are institutions that undergo a number of reorganizations, or that continually must change the technology they employ. or that have markets that are subject to fads, whims, and other essentially unpredictable changes.

One can summarize the applicability of MBO as follows. If the organization's environment:

1. changes too slowly, the costs of installing and maintaining MBO exceed its usefulness
2. changes too rapidly, MBO is unable to track the environmental changes quickly enough and thus is unsuccessful
3. changes at an in-between rate, then the benefits from MBO outweigh its costs.

Other problems arise if the MBO system is not well integrated with other, major organizational programs; these programs, being established and accepted, dominate and eventually MBO fades away. Examples of other major organizational programs are budgeting, production planning, and project scheduling. "Integration" of MBO with them may merely consist of ensuring that their respective time periods coincide, not overlap; that responsibilities and goals mesh; and that the workload pattern is smooth, not characterized by peaks and valleys.

Top management must also be sensitive to the needs of their middle managers, lest they destroy the MBO system from the inside out. A typical fear of middle managers is that their proper authority will be eroded by the MBO system and that they are being asked to delegate some of their legitimate power to incompetent subordinates. The middle managers will have to be reassured that it is normal for their

subordinates to make mistakes, that is partly
their duty to select and train subordinates
who can assume and properly exercise responsibility, and that the MBO system involves a
modification in their authority, not an ero-
sion of it—it will just take a different
form.

Other complaints from middle managers are
that the MBO program is very time consuming
because of all the individual meetings which
must be held and that it involves large
amounts of paperwork due to the records which
must be kept (and transmitted to higher-level
supervisors) of the goal agreements. A partial
rebuttal to the first argument is that the increase in time spent with each person should
not be that great, if the person was truly an
effective supervisor before the MBO program
was started. However, it is true that MBO is
costly in terms of time and paperwork.

Since one of the cornerstones of MBO is objectively verifiable goals, it may develop
that the MBO program shifts attention to focus
upon the quantitatively measurable aspects of
people's performances. This is not desirable.
Ways must be implemented to assess the more
qualitative aspects of human behavior, to incorporate that into the performance review,
and to use that information in deciding about
raises and other rewards which might be distributed. To narrow attention to the quantifi-
able is to invite displacement from the ends
to the means.

REPORTS FROM PRACTICE

In spite of that formidable list of problems,
several firms report successful use of MBO.
Most studies of MBO have been descriptive
(e.g., Odiorne, 1965). There are only four
cases in which the benefits and costs of MBO
have been carefully measured and evaluated,
either behaviorally or with respect to performance. Interestingly enough, all four of these

cases concerned large, United States based, manufacturing-oriented firms, even though MBO can be used with marketing firms (see Etzel and Ivancevich, 1974, for such a proposal) and has been used abroad (see Carroll and Tosi, 1973, pp. 12-13), as well as in a variety of nonfirms (see Ivancevich, 1974, p. 563, for references to its use in medical institutions, school systems, and governmental agencies). Despite the wide application of MBO, only the findings from the four studies are sketched.

The first careful empirical study of MBO was done by Meyer, Kay, and French (1965) at the General Electric Corporation. They were fortunate in being able to contrast the MBO group (they called their variant of MBO "Work Planning and Review," so they referred to their group as the WPR group) with those using the traditional performance appraisal system at G.E. They found no change in the attitudes of those managers using the traditional system, but the WPR managers evidenced attitude change in favorable directions on items such as "the ability of their managers to plan," "the extent to which their managers made use of their abilities and experience," "the value of the performance discussions they had with their managers," and "the degree to which they felt goals were what they should be." From these findings, Meyer, Kay, and French concluded that improvements in performance were much more likely to emanate from managers of WPR groups than from those continuing to use the traditional system.

In a second study, at the Purex Corporation, Raia (1965) studied another variant of MBO called "goal setting and self control." He discovered that under MBO managers were more aware of Purex's goals and that specific goals were being set in previously unexplored areas. Before MBO was introduced, productivity at Purex was declining at the rate of .4% per month. After MBO was started, productivity turned around and began increasing at .3% per month. In a follow-up study of the same program,

Raia (1966) found continuing increases in productivity, better analysis of problem areas, higher levels of goal attainment, improved communications, and improvements in managerial planning and control. However, he also found that some managers felt there was an overemphasis on measurable goals, such as production goals. Other managers also felt that the program was "easy to beat." And some managers felt that the MBO program did not motivate people to improve their performance since the goal-setting program was not clearly tied to the reward system. (See also Raia, 1974.)

Carroll and Tosi (1973) have studied the introduction of MBO into the Black & Decker Manufacturing Company. They found that those managers who were more positively disposed toward the MBO program tended to set more difficult goals, and perceived with greater clarity the importance and relevance of goals. They also found that the higher the frequency of feedback, the more satisfaction there was with the MBO program and the greater the degree of goal accomplishment. However, some managers reported that they felt that the MBO program was never really used to its full potential. Others noted that there was a strong emphasis on the procedure to be followed, to the detriment of the purpose behind or the substance of the MBO program. From their study of the perceived advantages, disadvantages, and suggestions for improving the MBO program, Carroll and Tosi devote chapters 3, 4, 5, and 6 and several appendices of their book to the important problem of properly implementing MBO in an ongoing organization. (Chapter 9 of Raia, 1974, is also addressed to that important topic.) For example (see Carroll and Tosi, 1973, p. 72), they recommend that the goals developed in the superior-subordinate negotiations should satisfy five classes of constraints:

1. They should be clear, concise, and unambiguous,

2. They should be accurate in terms of what is actually desired,
3. They should be consistent with organizational policies, procedures, and plans,
4. They should be within the competence of the person,
5. They should be interesting, motivating, and challenging, if at all possible.

Finally, Ivancevich (1974) studied the introduction of MBO into two of six plants of the Palos manufacturing corporation, using a third plant for comparative purposes. In all, he studied over a three year period the performance of roughly 2,500 subordinates of 181 MBO-involved supervisors in production and marketing departments. In one of the two experimental plants (P_1), MBO was simply instituted. In the other experimental plant (P_2), not only was MBO introduced, but also various reinforcements were given during the third year of the study—letters from high executives thanking the supervisors for carrying out the worthwhile MBO program, group meetings in which managers supported MBO, memos from the personnel unit indicating who could help the supervisors with their MBO problems, a letter from the president of Palos indicating that MBO would be continued in the future. The results of the study were different for the three different plants. The comparison plant showed no significant changes in various indices of either its production and marketing departments. The production department of the P_1 plant (MBO only) typically showed early improvement, in the first year or two, but then it tailed off to no significant change (the exception was that the grievance rate grew significantly.*less* favorable for the firm); the marketing department in P_1 consistently showed significant, though small, improvements in sales performance, sales per visit, and marketing potential. By contrast, the P_2 plant (MBO plus reinforcers) not only showed large significant improvements in the three marketing indices, it also had large, favorable, and significant improvements to all four indices in the production area (quantity, quality, grievance rate, absenteeism)—not only during the one- to two-year period but also at the end of the three years of the study.

The implication of the Ivancevich study is that it is a fourth datum indicating the advantage of MBO, and it also indicates that there may be ways to augment and increase the usefulness of MBO as well as suggesting that there may be situations or conditions under which MBO would not be effective. For example, the literature on MBO does not contain an adequate discussion of the role of unions, which should be supremely important since MBO is usually directed at the lowest-level employees. One suspects that for these four studies of the implementation of MBO either there was no union in effect or there was a very progressive or nontruculent union (lacking information, one leans toward the former explanation). As management by objectives receives more thorough investigation, its limitations and promise will become more definite. Currently, the range of usefulness of MBO is not completely clear.

In conclusion, management by objectives has demonstrated its usefulness in practice. It cannot be applied to a company in a cookbook fashion, but when the necessary conditions are met and a degree of sensitivity is used, most organizations can benefit from MBO.

REFERENCES

Carroll, S. J., Jr., and Tosi, H. L., Jr. *Management by Objectives—Applications and Research*. New York: Macmillan, 1973.

Drucker, P. *The Practice of Management*. New York: Harper, 1954.

Etzel, M. J., and Ivancevich, J. M. "Management by Objectives in Marketing: Philosophy, Process, and Problems." *Journal of Marketing* 38, no. 4 (October 1974): 47-55.

House, R. J. "A Path Goal Theory of Leader Effectiveness." *Administrative Science Quarterly* 16, no. 3 (September 1971): 321-338.

Hulin, C. L., and Blood, M. R. "Job Enlargement, Individual Differences, and Worker Responses." *Psychological Bulletin* 69, no. 1 (1968): 41-53.

Ivancevich, J. M. "Changes in Performance in a Management by Objective Program." *Administrative Science Quarterly* 19, no. 4 (December 1974): 563-574.

Likert, R. *New Patterns of Management*. New York: McGraw-Hill, 1961.

Levinson, H. "Management by Whose Objectives?" *Harvard Business Review* 48 (July-August 1970): 125-134.

McGregor, D. *The Human Side of Enterprise*. New York: McGraw-Hill, 1960.

Meyer, H. H., Kay, E., and French, J.P.R. "Split Roles in Performance Appraisal." *Harvard Business Review* 43 (January-February 1965): 123-129.

Morse, N. C., and Reimer, E. "The Experimental Change of a Major Organizational Variable." *Journal of Abnormal and Social Psychology* 52 (1956): 120-129.

Odiorne, G. *Management by Objectives*. New York: Pitman, 1965.

Pfeffer, J. *Organizational Design*. Arlington Heights, Ill.: AHM Publishing Corporation, 1978.

Pounds, W. F. "The Process of Problem Finding." *Industrial Management Review* (Fall 1969): 1-19.

Raia, A. P. "Goal Setting and Self Control." *Journal of Management Studies* (February 1965): 34-53.

Raia, A. P. "A Second Look at Goals and Controls." *California Management Review* 8 (Summer 1966): 49-58.

Raia, A. P. *Managing by Objectives*. Glenview, Ill.: Scott, Foresman, 1974.

Ridgway, V. F. "Dysfunctional Consequences of Performance Measurements." *Administrative Science Quarterly* 1, no. 2 (September 1956): 240-247.

Varney, G. H. "Management by Objective: Making it Work." *Supervisory Management* 40 (January 1972): 24-30.

6

Organizational Problem-Solving

Recall from chapter 4 that *decisions* were defined to be situations in which an action is to be selected from a number of alternative possibilities, and that *problems* were defined to be situations in which some past, current, or prospective future state is not in accord with what is desired. When something "bad" happens, such as an accident, catastrophe or crisis, the "problem" is to eliminate the "badness." That is, it is the presence of the "badness" that is not in accord with what is desired. Usually, problem-solving is the precursor to decision-making. The end result of problem-solving is to identify the cause of the difficulty or to develop alternative ways of rectifying the situation. Decision-making is used to select a "best" course of action to follow.

Also recall from chapter 4 that there are four (ideal) types of situations: static

routine, continuing routine, static novel, and
continuing novel. The latter two cases are addressed in this chapter, namely, those situations for which SOPs fail.

Typically, problem-solving processes traverse
three stages—recognition, formulation, and
search. During the problem-recognition phase,
the problem is initially encountered, sketched
out enough so it is "understood," and delegated so that some organizational unit will
cope with it. The result of the problem-formu-
lation phase is a problem description that has
been fleshed out enough so the solver can begin searching (the problem may be reformulated
as the solver explores more and learns more
about the problem) and can recognize that a
solution has been found. The search phase is
concerned with attempting to discover the cause
of the problem or with taking steps to rectify
the difficulty. Several models of the search
process will be examined later in this chapter.

Let us examine the following hypothetical
situation in detail to highlight several
important facets of the problem-solving process. Consider the "father and sons" problem:

> A father and two sons are on one bank of a river.
> There is a boat, but the capacity of the boat is 200
> pounts. The father weighs 200 pounds, and each of
> the sons weighs 100 pounds. How do the three of them
> cross to the other side of the river?

This is "recognized" to be a problem since the
given state (what is), namely, their presence
on one side of the river, does not match the
goal state (what is desired), namely, their
presence on the other side of the river. One
"formulation" of the problem is that the given
state can be symbolized as

where F = father, S = one son, B = boat; the goal state could likewise be symbolized as

and the operators could be symbolized as

$\longrightarrow$ (No operation)

$\xrightarrow{1S}$ (Put one son in the boat and cross)

$\xrightarrow{2S}$ (Put two sons in the boat and cross)

$\xrightarrow{F}$ (Put the father in the boat and cross)

Then to "search" out a solution to this problem, we can use the state transition diagrams from chapter 1.

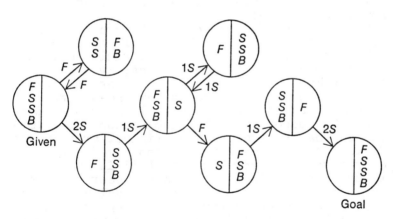

Observe that two "mistakes" were made, in that states were visited that are not on the solution path.

There are many important features to observe about the father-and-sons task and its solution.

First, it is only a problem for those who believe that the difference between the given
and goal states is material and important. If
you regard it as merely an inconsequential
brain teaser or puzzle, there is no problem.
Likewise, the definition of organizational
problems is *entirely* subjective.

Second, if one accepts the father-and-sons
task as a problem, the exhibited formulation
of it is only one possibility. Other formulations allow other operators, such as swimming,
building a bigger boat, constructing a bridge,
looking for a narrower part of the river, and
so on; and allow other state descriptions; for
example, somebody stays behind or seeks an
alternative route. Likewise, organizational
problems admit multiple formulations. It
should be recognized that problem formulation
constrains search by defining the domain in
which search is permissible. It should also be
noted that problems can be formulated in such
a way so as to prevent solution. This sometimes
occurs in organizations out of ignorance, and
sometimes it is done deliberately to punish,
annoy, or ridicule.

Third, problems are solved through a *process*,
not through some S-R mechanism. In addition to
the phases of recognition and formulation, the
search phase itself is a process, even permitting backups from erroneous branches to occur,
as happened twice in the father-and-son task.

Fourth, the search phase is largely dependent
upon the outcomes of the recognition and formulation phases (suppose the original problem was
defined to be "the river is too wide" and
operators were formulated to fill it in, dam
it up, reroute it, etc.). In the search phase,
the operators as formulated are applied to the
problem elements as formulated, beginning with
the given state as defined and terminating when
the goal state, as defined, is reached.

PROBLEM RECOGNITION AND FORMULATION

Problem recognition occurs when an individual

or group within the organization perceives a difference between some aspect of the organization's state and some preferred, more desirable state. Pounds (1969) notes that the former information can either originate from outside the organization (e.g., a supplier raising prices drastically) or internally. In the latter case, the problem could be discovered either through the analysis of historical data (e.g., sales quotas not being met), of data about current operations (e.g., an interruption in production), or of projections of the organization's probable future behavior (e.g., forecast of a dip in the company's earnings).

Pounds goes on to note that problems are recognized because of the existence of a "model" of the relevant situation—a "model" which allows one to conclude that something untoward was occurring, is occurring, or will occur. (A "model" is a simplified theory of the variables and their interaction that allows one to "understand" a situation.) Based on the assumption of continuity of historical relationships, there is a wide variety of historical models (e.g., in costs, product quality, departmental attitudes). Violation of the historical condition leads to a problem being recognized. Similarly, there are a number of planning models, extra-organizational models (from competitors, trade associations, governments), scientific and engineering models, and models from other people and units within the same organization. Whenever one of the explanations from the models is not met (plans fail, competitors are more successful, the firm is below industry average, the firm breaks some law, manufacturing attempts to violate some physical law, a higher-level manager requests a report and supporting analysis), a problem is revealed. (However, contrary to Pounds' position, Braybrooke and Lindblom, 1963, argue that no model is needed to uncover the existence of problems. They note that public policy problems arise and are dealt with without ever admitting one model as "the" correct view of the situation.)

Once the existence of a problem has been uncovered, it is developed enough so that it can
be properly categorized. Should it be solved
by the unit that discovered it or does it
properly belong elsewhere in the organization?
Does the unit that discovered the problem have
the authority to cope with it or should it be
transmitted to higher echelons in the organization? Is the problem relatively unimportant or
should news of its existence be communicated to
others in the organization?

Once the problem has been adequately recognized, problem formulation activities dominate.
Since problems are differences between "what
is" (or "what was" or "what will be") and "what
is (or will be) desired," these activities are,
largely, to characterize the problem along
those dimensions. Ideally, both the current
(or past, or future) state and the desired
state are carefully elaborated, so the essential differences between them can be studied.
For example, upon more careful examination,
it may be determined that the desired state is
not really that desirable, or that the difference between the two is smaller than was originally thought. Other reasons for carefully
specifying the differences are to help identify
the search process to be used and where the
chosen search process should begin.

Another consideration in the problem-formula-
tion phase is the determination of what type
of organizational unit the problem shall be
delegated to: an individual, an existing committee, or an ad hoc task force. If one of the
latter two is selected, the size of the group
needs to be determined—the usual arguments
favor a group of odd parity (so a majority will
always exist, i.e., so ties are proscribed), of
at least five (so a viable minority position is
possible), and relatively smaller groups so
action can be consummated quickly. (See Shull,
Delbecq, and Cummings, 1970, ch. 5.) These
arguments point toward "five" as being the
optimal size for a small group.

The decision as to whether a group or a person should work on the problem is made by considering several aspects of the problem, the person responsible for its solution, and other relevant people in the organization. For example, if the problem is very complex, or if it is important that the possibility for error be minimized, or if it is desirable to obtain a broad degree of commitment to the eventual solution, these factors argue for using a group to solve the problem. However, if the problem is simple, needs a quick solution, and requires a clear assignment of responsibility, these factors argue for using an individual to solve the problem. If a locus of expertise can be identified, either in an individual, an existing group (e.g., a staff group; see chapter 8), or diffusely throughout an organization (e.g., in various members of the organization who can be assembled into an ad hoc task force), then the problem will be assigned where the expertise can be identified. Other factors that mitigate against assigning a problem to an individual are the need to communicate rapidly the problem, the solution, and the reasoning to many segments of the organization; the need to motivate, unify, and direct the energies of many facets of the organization; and the need to recognize the political realities that exist in the organization. (For more details on these factors operating in an organizational context, see March and Simon, 1948, pp. 180-182; or see Blau and Scott, 1962, pp. 116-128.)

One factor that has not been discussed is the relative risk or conservatism of groups versus individuals. This is still an open question due to the lack of consensus on an adequate definition of "risk."

Other research has shown that "brainstorming" (see Osborn, 1957) is usually not effective in maximizing the number of alternatives produced or in maximizing the quality of the alternatives (see Taylor, Berry, and Block,

1958; and Rotter and Portugal, 1969). Instead, the preferred procedure is to construct "pseudo-groups": Rather than giving the problem to a group of, say, nine, and letting them brainstorm, give the problem to the nine individuals, let them produce alternatives in isolation from one another, then pool the results and discard any redundancies.

SEARCH PROCESSES

Now that the problem has been formulated, it remains to search it out. Of course, the definition of the problem may change as the search process unfolds. Four broad types of search processes descriptive of actual organizational problem-solving will be discussed: (1) reactive, (2) circumscribed, (3) opportunistic and (4) idiomatic. In the next section, I will give prescriptive, or normative, models of the search process.

REACTIVE SEARCH

Reactive search processes are those that respond to dissatisfaction. As the magnitude of the dissatisfaction increases, the propensity to search and the intensity of the search increase. Mathematical, graphical, and verbal models of the reactive search process may be found in March and Simon (1958, pp. 47-52). Once the dissatisfaction is reduced, the search process terminates. The reactive search process begins in the vicinity of the supposed cause of (or at least factors strongly related to) the dissatisfaction.

For example, Cyert and March (1963, ch. 5) describe the probable behaviors of business firms in duopolistic market situations. The firm sets its aspirations on profits, estimates what its competitor will do, and then projects the revenues it expects to realize and the costs it expects to endure. From this, it can calculate its expected profit; if expected

profit is below desired profit, this firm has
a problem. The problem is attacked by sequentially searching along various lines. First,
planned one-time-only expenditures are sought
(e.g., expansion plans) and, if any are found,
they are eliminated. Then, expected profits
are recalculated to see if the problem still
exists, and, if it does, whether it is of
diminished magnitude. If the problem still exists and still is of sufficient size to merit
attention, the second step is taken, which is
to attempt to reduce other costs, but keeping
the quantity produced the same as previously
forecast. This could be by attempting to increase efficiency (to cut the per unit costs),
to lay off personnel, to seek cheaper material,
and so on. Expected profits are recalculated.
If the problem still exists, the third step is
taken, which involves finding ways to increase
revenue (e.g., increase advertising, modify
prices, market a new product, improve quality).
Again, profit projections are remade. If the
problem persists, the fourth, final, definitive
search occurs: Aspirations on profits (and
aspirations on other variables) are lowered
until the problem vanishes, by definition, from
the organization. Aspirations can always be
lowered sufficiently so that the expected level
of performance is always "near" the desired
level of performance.

Since one can always define problems out of
existence (by changing what the desired state
is considered to be), why is this used only as
a last resort? For that matter, why do these
four steps appear in the sequence as they do?
The answers are because the problematical elements to the problem are *not* originally perceived to lie in the definition of the desired
state, but rather are with the current (or
past, or future) state. Only when all responsible attempts at modifying the current state
fail to remove the problem is the problem perceived to be with the aspirations. Finally,
the reasons for the order of the search are
that it progresses from elements over which the

organization has a great deal of control (expansion plans) to those which may be relatively uncontrollable (how much of the product is purchased). Organizations are also much more cognizant of their cost functions than they are of the characteristics of the demand for their product. Lastly, it is easier to effect changes within the organization than in the marketplace.

CIRCUMSCRIBED SEARCH

Circumscribed search is much like reactive search in that it is stimulated by dissatisfaction, but circumscribed search is considerably simpler than reactive search. In a sense, reactive search is exhaustive; the search progresses until the problem disappears. In circumscribed search, boundaries around and limitations to the search process are tacitly or explicitly imposed. The motivation is to simplify the search process so that (1) a response can be quickly forthcoming, and (2) proper account is taken of the limited information-processing capabilities of the people involved in the problem and in the searching. Thus circumscribed search is a subset of reactive search.

Cyert and March (1963, ch. 6) narrate three concepts descriptive of the search procedures used by organizations: Problematic Search, Quasi-Resolution of Conflict, and Uncertainty Avoidance. The idea behind Problemistic Search is that the search process is problem-stimulated and problem-oriented. Searching *only* occurs in response to problems; it does not originate out of scientific curiosity or random thrashing about or for any other reason. The search process is directed toward solving the problem. No other avenues uncovered are explored. Once the problem is solved, the searching terminates. The search process is rather simple-minded; search begins in the vicinity of the symptoms of the problem and only expands outward when the symptoms fail to suggest a solution. Finally, the search process is biased in accordance with the perceptions of those conducting the search. The phenomenon of "selective perception" is well known (see, e.g., Dearborn and Simon, 1958; or Jabes, 1978). Similarly, personal and organizational biases will suggest the order in which elements are searched and how those elements will be evaluated.

The concept Quasi-Resolution of Conflict refers to the organization's attempt to handle the number of necessarily interconnected problems by which it is always confronted. Since the organization never completely solves its problems nor is it able to consider comprehensively all of the simultaneous interdependencies in its problems, the process is called Quasi-Resolution of Conflict. The goals and aspirations of the firm are developed and are treated in relative isolation from one another (e.g., revenue forecasts are created independently from cost standards, though profit aspirations are reconciled against both projected revenues and expected costs). To help delimit the search process it is typical to formulate goals, objectives, and aspirations as satisficing type of criteria and to assign single goals to organizational subunits, so problems get searched from only one vantage point. However, the most singular behavior is the sequential and independent attention accorded to problems and goals. That is, the firm may have a pressing liquidity problem and to solve it may sell off much inventory. Then in the next time period, the firm may have a stockout problem and to solve it may add more workers and schedule more overtime. Thus in the next time period the firm may have a cost-of-sales problem and may solve it by instituting a severe cost-cutting campaign. This in turn may cause a revenue problem, and so on.

Observe that each problem is treated independently of the others, although they are clearly related. Observe further that the search for a solution to each problem is limited by

not considering the implications of the solution for other parts or aspects of the organization.

Organizations, and the personnel in them,
disdain uncertainty in their multifaceted environment. (*Uncertainty* refers to *all* of the
factors in an organization's existence that can
vary unpredictably: whether employees will show
up at work, whether machines will function,
whether customers will make purchases, whether
civil war will break out, etc.) The reasons are
many: the potential for error, for financial
loss, for loss of face, for anxiety and its
associated psychological discomfort, and so on.
Search processes are further circumscribed by
Uncertainty Avoidance. There are two noteworthy
manifestations of Uncertainty Avoidance: the
use of SOPs and negotiation with the environment. Using SOPs clearly circumscribes the
search process as the alternatives are already
specified, at least up to a parameter setting.
As seen previously in chapter 4, organizations
tend initially to treat all problems as though
they are of the static routine type. Thus, the
use of SOPs is to avoid, indeed even to deny
the existence of, uncertainty, and thus to delimit search.

However, once the existence of uncertainty
has been acknowledged by an organization, the
issue remains of how the organization shall
cope with it. The organization attempts to
minimize the uncertainty it faces by negotiating with its environment. Internally, this results in budgets, five-year plans, inventories,
multi-year labor contracts, and policies. Externally, the organization attempts to secure
multi-year supply arrangements, future agreements, long-term debt, and is likely to band
together, formally or tacitly, with similar organizations in order to form "industry associations." By convention or fiat, agreement is
reached on standards, price lines, sale dates,
and so on. In the extreme case of uncertainty
avoidance, there is collusion in restraint of
trade.

By the procedures described under Problemistic Search, Quasi-Resolution of Conflict,
and Uncertainty Avoidance, the search processes evoked during problem-solving by organizations are effectively circumscribed, delimited,
and curtailed.

OPPORTUNISTIC SEARCH

A third model of search is opportunistic
search. The idea is that the organization
searches for opportunities and, when the organization finds what it perceives to be an opportunity, investigates it thoroughly. Opportunistic search is similar to reactive search,
except that it is a movement *toward* something
(an opportunity) rather than a movement *away*
from something (a problem). Organizations usually label as "opportunities" those situations
which (1) will help achieve a goal (e.g., a
project which allows the firm to grow) or allow
more of a goal to be achieved (e.g., a project
which permits faster growth); (2) will remove,
reduce, or negate a constraint (e.g., an action
which lessens inventory requirements), thus
providing indirect assistance to achieving (1);
or (3) will bar or diminish a foreseeable,
prospective, or projected constraint (e.g., a
plan which frees cash three years hence), thus
indirectly aiding (2). From these definitions
of "opportunity," opportunistic search is concerned with uncovering or exploring more fully
action alternatives which advance the organization's goals or which mitigate constraints.
Carter (1971) describes the search behavior of
top-level executives in a small northeastern
computer time leasing firm as being opportunistic.

Clearly, opportunistic search may be triggered by partial findings from reactive, circumscribed, or even idiomatic search. (In a
similar vein, any of these search procedures
may be evoked and used defensively, as a ratio-
nalization, from any other of the procedures.)
However, the most singularly pristine version

of opportunistic search occurs when an organization views one of its constraints as too
binding (organizational goals may also be
viewed as constraints; see Simon, 1964) and
embarks upon a search for ways to lessen that
grip. For self-motivated opportunistic search
to occur, the constraint must neither be too
loose, which might result in insufficient motivation to search, nor be too tight, lest de-
spair terminate the search process.

IDIOMATIC SEARCH

The fourth and final class is called idiomatic search. In this model, the search is guided
by the idiosyncratic characteristics of the
individuals participating in the process. Without knowledge of those characteristics, it is
impossible to predict or understand the search
process in detail. Furthermore, as the organizational coalition coping with the problem
shifts, the set of operative personal features
will likewise be modified.

For example, Carter (1971) describes two
other search cases in this same firm which meet
the requirements of idiomatic search. In one
case, a search was conducted by one of the
top-level executives for a solution to a problem provided that the solution would advance
the career of that person. That is, the problem-solver searched to satisfy his own goals
and not the organization's objectives.

In Carter's second case, search was both initiated and conducted to satisfy the personal
beliefs of the solver about the way in which
business was done, the type of business the
firm was in, the manner in which the firm was
organized, and so on. That is, the search was
due to personal perceptions and beliefs.

A third example of idiomatic search is to be
found in Braybrooke and Lindblom's (1963) analysis of government policy-making. According to
them, alternative policies are analyzed through
"successive limited comparisons," that is, a

proposed policy is examined for its marginal
effects or differences from the current policy,
status quo, or against other proposed policies.
A "good" policy is found when various analysts
agreed upon one, and they typically do so without agreeing on either (1) what goals the unit
should hold, or (2) that the agreed-upon policy
is the best means for achieving those goals.
Since "good" policies are discovered using
"successive limited comparisons" in conjunc-
tion with indigenous personal preference functions, this too is an example that fits the
mold of idiomatic search.

A fourth instance of idiomatic search is to
be found in the "garbage can" model of organizations originated by Cohen, March, and Olsen
(1972). The garbage can model posits that
organizations are loose collections of participants, problems, solutions, decisions, choices,
tools, and technologies. That is, organizations
are a kind of melting pot, in which people
come and go; when they are present, they have
their pet solutions, their favorite choices,
and their preferred tools, techniques, and
technologies. Problems arise almost spontane-
ously and decision situations are latently
and implicitly recognized. Rather quickly,
solutions are attached to problems and choices
are assigned to decisions; the remainder of
the process is to justify and to rationalize
the assignments that have already been made.
Similarly, as new problem-solving tools and
technologies become available, they are advanced as the "best way" to approach the currently extant problem and decision situations.
Also, each participant has an "energy pool"
or "reservoir" to draw from, and each situation
has an energy level associated with it (i.e.,
the amount of energy necessary to cope with
it). Then there are two ways in which search
on a problem can be terminated (according to
the garbage can model): (1) the energy requirement of the problem has been met—it is
"solved" through some mechanism; or (2) the

participants run out of energy and searching
on the problem is concluded—in some cases the
problem may be defined to be "solved."

Obviously, in the garbage can model, the
search process is quite dependent upon the
current confluence of problems, decisions,
participants, and their solutions, choices,
tools, energy levels, techniques, and technologies. It is also clear that the garbage
can model, and the idiomatic search paradigm
in general, is distinct from the other three
search models. The four search models offer
differential predictions about the *outcome*
or the result of the searching, but rather dis-
tinctive predictions are made about the *process*
or method of conducting the searching. There
is enough empirical evidence to lend credence
to each of the four types of models. However,
we do not yet know which (indeed, if any) of
the models is empirically superior. It may be
that some as yet undiscovered factor accounts
for which search process is used, or that the
truth is some mild blend of these four (and
possibly other) models, or that there is some
single, general search model that accounts for
these four rather specialized models.

The four search models discussed in this
section detail how the search process is conducted. But to explicate organizational problem-solving fully, it is necessary to couple
the concept of the search process with information of the locus and depth of the search. In
general, the locus and depth of search depends
upon three primary factors: the nature of the
difficulty or opportunity, the time available,
and the amount of other resources marshaled
for the problem.

The centrality of the difficulty or opportunity to the set or organizational objectives
helps determine the amount of attention that
will be accorded it, that is, the depth of
the search. The more central, the more search
(ceteris paribus), and conversely. For example,
a product-producing profit-oriented firm will
usually react intensely to a project downturn

in profits (because profits are central to its goals), whereas governmental agencies ordinarily pay scant attention to problems of inefficiency because efficieny is not central to their goals).

The nature of the difficulty or opportunity also determines where the search process originates, although the search may eventually travel far afield. For example, with a marketing problem, the search may begin with the salesmen's efforts, go to product characteristics, the production department's ability to adhere to a delivery schedule, and the budget for advertising.

It is hard to overemphasize the dependence of the locus of the search upon the definition of the problem. As an illustration, consider a firm that is experiencing symptoms of insufficient sales. The way that a problem is crystallized around those symptoms will largely dictate where the search occurs. If the problem is defined as "sluggish economy," the production rate may be reduced or other cost-saving measures investigated. If the problem is defined as "not price competitive," ways to cut quality may be sought. If the problem is generally considered to be "inept marketing," then depending upon the details of its definition, the problem may be searched along the lines of either reorganizing that function, or retraining the personnel, or firing a number of people.

As a "real" example of this, consider the case of Sam Adams (1975), analyst for the CIA investigating the size of the North Vietnamese and Viet Cong armies. His analyses produced answers some three times larger than the "official" estimates; this discrepancy posed a problem to the CIA. (It is, incidentally, a case of reactive search—the CIA reacted to the dissatisfaction produced by having two quite dissimilar estimates as to the size of the enemy's army.) However, instead of defining the problem to be one of learning what the true size was, the CIA chose to define the old official estimate as the truth and to define the problem as getting Mr. Adams to accept this version of the truth. More and more pressures were put on him until he "voluntarily" chose to resign from the agency. Note carefully how the locus of search depends upon how the problem is defined.

The time available to solve the problem, that is, to produce *some* solution to the problem, also affects the search's locus and depth. Naturally, the less time, the shallower the search. Also, the less time available, the more likely it is that the search will be restricted to the symptoms of the problem, rather than its necessary causes. When time is restricted, the problem-solver must rely upon his intuition as to where a solution lies.

Finally, the amount of other resources available for the problem-solving efforts also create an impact upon the locus and depth of search. These other resources include "release time" for a manager to investigate the problem, the possibility of using committees, task forces, teams or staff groups, and computer time. The more these other resources are available, the deeper and broader the search can be.

NORMATIVE SEARCH PROCEDURES

Some empirical evidence and much anecdotal evidence teaches us that an appallingly high percentage of organizational problems is solved by SOP, flight, avoidance, and oversight. To help rectify these unfortunate conditions, several authors have developed prescriptive theories to allow better, in some cases optimal, problem-solving search procedures to be used. For example, Hyman and Anderson (1965) have developed a set of eight precepts to be followed by an individual while he is solving a problem. Two of their precepts are (1) "Explore the environment. Vary the temporal and spatial arrangements of the materials," (p. 37); and (2) "When stuck, change your representational system. If a concrete representation isn't working, try an abstract one, and vice versa" (p. 40). The Hyman and Anderson precepts are oriented toward problem-solving in general, based upon general characteristics of people. Two somewhat more specialized normative search theories for organizational problem-solving will be considered in more detail: The first concerns an individual manager in the organization, and the second relates to the organizational response to a complex, novel situation.

According to Kepner and Tregoe (1965), a truly rational manager engages in a sequential, three-phase activity pattern: problem-solving, decision-making, and planning (or potential problem analysis). The theory is that problems will occasionally arise in an organizational setting; the purpose of the problem-solving phase is to find the cause, or the most likely cause, of the problem. Then the aim of the decision-making phase is to select the best action to alleviate the problem. Finally, the planning or potential problem analysis phase is to anticipate what problems may occur and to develop actions to prevent, correct, or curtail those potential problems.

It is important in the Kepner-Tregoe procedure to distinguish among symptoms, problems, and causes. *Symptoms* are merely observations of facts. *Problems* are differences between what is (i.e., symptoms) and what is desired. *Causes* are those factors or forces that result in differences between what is and what is desired.

For example, a machine may be producing widgets at the rate of 50 per hour; that is a symptom. If the desired production rate is 180 per hour, that defines a problem. Via their problem-solving phase, the cause of that problem is to be found.

In the problem-solving phase, Kepner and Tregoe recommend that a seven-step procedure be followed in order to find the cause, or the most probable cause, of the problem. They report much success with their procedures in a wide variety of organizational settings. The

seven steps of the problem-solving method
are:

1. Establish a standard of performance, that
   is, a desired state of affairs.
2. Determine that there is a material difference between the actual state and the desired state.
3. Carefully specify what the problem *is*—what
   it is, where it is, when it is, and to what
   extent it is.
4. So as to comprehend the problem completely,
   also carefully specify what it is *not*—what
   it is not, where it does not occur, when it
   does not occur, and to what extent it does
   not occur.
5. Identify the underlying changes that have
   occurred in the problematic situation (the
   deviation between what is desired and what
   is happening can only be due to some change
   in the situation).
6. Deduce, scientifically, possible causes of
   the deviation from the relevant changes in
   the problematic situation.
7. The most likely cause of the problem is the
   one that explains the most facts in the
   specification of the problem.

   Suppose for the case of the balky machine
that the problem-solving phase reveals the
cause of the poor production rate is that several crucial parts are wearing out. Then there
are several alternative actions that could be
taken:

- Make do until it wears out completely.
- Replace the parts immediately.
- Replace the entire machine.
- Simply perform a maintenance on the machine.

There are also several important values and
criteria present:

- Get production rate up to 180 units per hour.
- Minimize machine downtime.
- Minimize financial outlay.

• Minimize overtime usage.
• Make maximum use of employee worktime.

How to combine these preferences and action
alternatives so as to best handle the original
problem is treated by the decision-making phase.
  Once the problem has been conceptually
solved, it remains to execute the seven steps
of their decision-making procedure so the best
way of implementing a solution may be chosen:

1. Establish the objectives of the decision.
2. Classify the objectives as to importance;
   basically, put them into the categories of
   "must" and "wants."
3. Develop alternative action possibilities.
4. Evaluate the alternatives against the objectives (Kepner and Tregoe recommend a
   weighted sum of features approach).
5. Make a tentative decision (it must meet all
   of the "musts" and, according to the
   weighted sums, more of the "wants" than
   other alternatives).
6. Explore the tentative decision for possible
   adverse consequences in areas such as
   people, organization, money, facilities and
   equipment, and output.
7. Control the effects of the final choice by
   taking actions sufficient to minimize possible adverse consequences and by making
   sure the actions decided upon are in fact
   carried out.

  Finally, after the problem has been solved
and after actions have been taken to counter-
mand it, the last item to be accomplished is
to execute the seven steps of the Kepner and
Tregoe potential problem analysis technique:

1. Determine what could go wrong; be wary of
   the new, complex, or unfamiliar, tight deadlines, critical sequences, involvement of
   multiple people, functions, or departments,
   and unclear responsibilities.
2. Describe each problem in specific terms,

that is, what, where, when, and to what degree it may occur.
3. Identify the riskiness of each problem; for
   Kepner and Tregoe, riskiness is a function
   of the seriousness of the problem and the
   probability of its occurrence. The riskiness of a problem is either "fatal" to the
   success of a decision, "damaging" but not
   fatal, or "annoying" but not damaging.
4. Learn the possible causes of each problem.
   Note carefully that in contrast to problem-
   solving, one does not learn *the* cause or
   the probable cause of the problem, but rather
   all *possible* causes.
5. Ascertain the probability of each possible
   cause; obviously, one only wants to attend
   to the most likely causes of the riskiest
   problems.
6. Figure out how the high-probability possible
   causes can be prevented or how their effects
   can be minimized.
7. Finally, for those potential problems of a
   serious nature for which preventative actions will not eliminate or mitigate them,
   contingency plans should be developed.

For the faulty widget-producing machine
again, potential problem analysis may suggest
that preventive maintenance or scheduled re-
placement of parts would be a good way of
coping with a problem likely to recur. It may
also suggest policies to handle raw materials
shortages, labor disturbance, or power inter-
ruptions.
The other normative problem-solving procedure to be studied is Swinth's (1971) Organizational Joint Problem-Solving System (OJPS).
The Kepner and Tregoe approach is directed
toward individual managers in the organization;
by contrast, OJPS is aimed at the entire organization.
The OJPS technique is to be used on complex
novel problems that affect the entire organization. Such problems have the following characteristics: The solution must meet a multitude

of objectives and satisfy a variety of participants. The problem is too complex to be understood or solved readily by any one person or
group; there is a need to pool information,
knowledge, and action from several sources.
The organization in which such problems arise
is typically organized into "centers"; where
there is a high degree of interdependence between them—the decisions made in one sphere
have implications and consequences for other
centers.

OJPS is most succinctly and accurately described by the author himself (Swinth, 1971,
p. B-71);

> Briefly, in OJPS a set of centers are linked together
> to deal with a problem. Search is initially conducted
> at the highest problem level to establish goals for
> the second level. The centers then search within
> their own components to meet these goals, ignoring
> for the moment between component interdependencies.
> The plan of action developed by any center and the
> rationale for it is then broadcast to other centers
> in the system. This permits inconsistencies between
> components to be resolved. The centers are also able
> to search coordinatively in new directions. The pro-
> cess of within component search, broadcasting of
> actions, and between component search and coordina-
> tion is iterated upon until an overall solution is
> found which is as close to the objectives of the
> task as the centers can come and is likewise internal-
> ly consistent between components and across levels.
> With this method of search it is not necessary for
> any one center or all centers to understand the whole
> problem, rather each need only interact with the
> others at the interfaces between them.

Observe that OJPS specifies how authority
and responsibility are to be distributed within the organization, how the processes of
search and coordination are to be carried out,
and how the major components of the system
(problem, participants, centers, environment)
are to be linked together to form an effective
problem-solving system.

The major shortcoming of any of the normative

theories of problem-solving search is the lack
of evidence of their superiority. There simply
is as yet no convincing proof that an individual, a manager, or an organization, armed with
one of these theories, is able to solve a problem it could not otherwise solve or is able to
produce a preferred solution to an already
solvable problem. There is anecdotal evidence
but neither is there careful empirical test nor
analytic proof that they are optimal or to be
preferred over current practices. Another problem with many of these theories is their failure to define their concepts and variables operationally. For many of them, their precepts,
rules, and principles could be applied many
different ways in a given practical situation,
and it is not clear what the authors ambiguous-
ly intended. Nevertheless, and somewhat more
charitably, there has to be a start somewhere;
improvements will be added to these theories
later on, but this progress is only forthcoming
because someone was willing to take the first
bold step. Furthermore, although it may not
currently be possible to prove the superiority
of these normatic theories, I believe they
represent considerable improvement over current
organizational practice. As prescriptive theories, they are very plausible.

REFERENCES

Adams, S. "Vietnam Cover-up:" Playing War with Numbers."
Harpers 250, no. 1500 (May 1975): 41ff.

Blau, P. M., and Scott, W. R. *Formal Organizations*.
San Francisco: Chandler, 1962.

Braybrooke, D., and Lindblom, C. E. *A Strategy of Decision*. New York: Free Press, 1963.

Carter, E. E. "The Behavioral Theory of the Firm and
Top-Level Corporate Decision." *Administrative Science
Quarterly* 16, no. 4 (December 1971): 413-428.

Cohen, M. D., March, J. G., and Olsen, J. P. "A Garbage Can Model of Organizational Choice." *Administrative Science Quarterly* 17, no. 1 (March 1972): 1-25.

Cyert, R. M., and March, J. G. *A Behavioral Theory of the Firm*. Englewood Cliffs, N.J.: Prentice-Hall, 1963.

Dearborn, D. C., and Simon, H. A. "Selective Perception: A Note on the Departmental Identification of Executives." *Sociometry* 21 (1958): 140-144.

Hyman, R., and Anderson, B. "Solving Problems." *Science and Technology* (September 1965): 36-41.

Jabes, J. *Individual Processes in Organizational Behavior*. Arlington Heights, Ill.: AHM Publishing Corporation, 1978.

Kepner, C. H., and Tregoe, B. B. *The Rational Manager*. New York: McGraw-Hill, 1965.

March, J. G., and Simon, H. A. *Organizations*. New York: Wiley, 1958.

Osborn, A. F. *Applied Imagination*. New York: Scribner's, 1957.

Pounds, W. F. "The Process of Problem Finding." *Industrial Management Review* (Fall 1969): 1-19.

Rotter, G. S., and Portugal, S. H. "Group and Individual Effects in Problem Solving." *Journal of Applied Industrial Psychology* 53 (1969): 338-341.

Shull, F. A., Jr., Delbecq, A. L., and Cummings, L. L. *Organizational Decision Making*. New York: McGraw-Hill, 1970.

Simon, H. A. "On the Concept of Organizational Goal." *Administrative Science Quarterly* 9 (June 1964): 1-22.

Swinth, R. L. "Organizational Joint Problem-Solving." *Management Science* 18, no. 2 (October 1971): B-68 to B-79.

Taylor, D. W., Berry, P. C., and Block, C. H. "Does Group Participation When Using Brainstorming Facilitate or Inhibit Creative Thinking?" *Administrative Science Quarterly* 3 (1958): 23-47.

Control and Coordination

Of prime interest to practicing administrators is how they may control the task and administrative activities of their subordinates and how they may coordinate their subordinates' behaviors. To control behavior is to supply direction for it and to monitor the ongoing behavior so as to ensure conformity to what the controller desires. To coordinate behaviors is to ensure that they are properly interleaved, sequenced, and timed so as to accomplish some global task completion. The control and coordination of behavior is clearly related to, but distinct from, the concept or organizational change (see Pfeffer, 1978). It is very apparent that the usual S-R paradigm is inadequate for the purposes of improving and understanding the effects of various control and coordination procedures. March and Simon 1958, ch. 3) describe the unintended, as well

as intended, responses to increased demand for
control in three "machine," that is, S-R models of bureaucracy (those of Merton, Selznick,
and Gouldner). Those people and units being
controlled and coordinated are not little
machines governed by simple S-R rules, they do
not exist isolated from the rest of the universe, they do possess a memory of the past,
and they do have their own sometimes changing
preferences for the future. As such, the process paradigm will be employed to examine alternative methods of controlling and coordinating organizational behavior, the necessary
preconditions for the successful use of these
methods, and the implications stemming from
their use and abuse.

Before examining several kinds of techniques
for controlling behavior in organizations, it
is instructive to consider the topics of control and coordination more broadly. One of
these issues is the question of why control
and coordination (for the duration of this
section, I shall simply use the term *control*
in place of that phrase) are in use at all in
organizations. After all, if one joins an organization, does he not accept its goals? (This
naive question ignores the myriad of motivations for joining organizations.) Control is
exercised for many, many reasons. Pragmatical-
ly, it is used to make task processes efficient
and to simplify informational and communication
requirements. Philosophically, it is used as
part of man's never-ending quest to seek understanding of his environment, to minimize his
uncertainty and anxiety, and to maximize his
satisfaction and self-actualization. Psychologically, it is used because some people enjoy
the dominant-submissive relationship (for some
illuminating studies of this, see Milgram,
1965), because knowledge of control procedures
such as rules and SOPs constitutes a base of
personal power, and because use of control procedures is a way of protecting oneself from
allegations of incompetence. Although

incomplete, this list highlights some of the reasons why control is used.

Another issue is the relationship between organizational goals and control procedures. Of course it is a truism that the clearer the goals are to the members of an organization, the less reliance there is, or needs to be, upon control procedures. However, when people do not know what they are doing, not only is more use made of control procedures, but there is also more elaboration. That is, in the absence of sure knowledge about purpose, not only is the system subjected to much control (relatively speaking) but also the amount of control employed increases over time—there are more forms, more inspections, more rules, and so on. This occurs partly out of a fear on the part of its top managers that the system will become autonomous, and partly from the recognition of the tie between control procedures and organizational goals. It is as if managers say to themselves "Since control procedures institutionalize organizational goals, maybe if enough control procedures are used we can infer what our goals are."

Thirdly, one of the most important control devices, at least as viewed from the perspective of subordinates, is the evaluation system, either an overt one or as assumed by the reward system (the amount and type of reward—or tangible value-laden prize, such as dollars or vacation time—someone receives is the most sincere form of evaluation he will ever get). To install or to operationalize further an evaluation system is to exhibit the desire to assert control. There are several possible problems with evaluation systems per se (I will discuss problems with power and authority-based control devices in general in the next section): They may be illegitimate, they may be invalid, and they may be accepted and supply meaningful information, but there may be no way to incorporate that knowledge to improve behavior. (For ways around these problems, see chapter 5 on Management by Objectives.)

Another issue is the question of the motivational assumptions behind the use of control procedures (see Jabes, 1978, ch. 3, for a deeper study of motivation). For example, McGregor (1960) posits two types of management styles, In order to be neutral about the study of them, he lables one as Theory X and the other as Theory Y. The Theory X manager assumes externally motivated subordinates and thus uses commensurate control devices (rules, authority, rewards, punishments, etc.). The Theory Y manager assumes internally motivated subordinates and so uses self-control devices such as goals, reasoning, and influence. McGregor's conclusion is that Theory X management is used too frequently, that Theory Y management could be put to more effective use.

A topic that has not received sufficient attention is the issue of the effects of organizational control on a person's individuality. How do greater and lesser amounts of control affect one's personality? What happens to a person when he is forced to conform to an activity that he believes is inefficient? Ineffective? Unwise? Unethical? Illegal? Are the various control procedures homogeneous with respect to these issues, or do some techniques amplify and others reduce the effects?

Finally, Etzioni (1961) has characterized the type of control procedures in use in organizations in order to develop a typology of organizations and to study changes in organizations. Briefly, there are coercive organizations (such as prisons and mental hospitals), utilitarian organizations (such as business and unions), normative organizations (such as churches and hospitals), and some mixed structures (such as an infantry combat unit). With this control typology, one can study such things as the types of involvement or psychological contact that are possible in organizations (alienation in the case of coercion, calculation in the case of utilitarianism, and morale in the case of normativism) and

the trends in overall control characteristics
(away from pure coercive and normative toward
combinations with utilitarian).

Now that you are aware of several broad issues in the study and use of control and
coordination procedures, a detailed examination of the major control devices is in order.

METHODS OF ACHIEVING CONTROL

REASONING AND LOGIC

One way to control behavior is simply to explain what is desired and the reasons for that
choice. This procedure requires that there be
a logical rationale for the desired behavior;
that the recipients of the statement and explanation can understand the reasoning; that
they accept the explanation; and that sufficient time is available for the communication
to take place, the information to be digested,
and the desired behaviors to be executed. If
any one of those factors is not present, use
of some other control device is indicated. And
of course, the fewer of those factors that obtain, the more usefulness of reasoning and
logic as a control device is mitigated.

If all the conditions are met, this method
is extremely powerful for supplying direction.
However, it is rare that all preconditions are
satisfied, for all directions necessarily contain an implicit or explicit reference to a
goal state, and goal state preferences cannot
be defended logically. The conditions necessary
for the use of reasoning and logic, conditions
such as mutual trust and respect and consensus
on goals, are not very frequently achieved in
complex, ongoing organizations. However, many
superiors pretend that those conditions are
met (since such conditions represent the normal
facade of organizational life) and use reasoning and logic as a control device—occasionally
resulting in surprising, unintended, and unanticipated behaviors by those being

"controlled." Another difficulty with this method is the prevalent possibility for pseudo-compliance—verbal assent but behavioral dissension.

In spite of the significant difficulties in properly applying this method, most managers use it exclusively or use it first, before falling back upon some other method (such as influence or authority). Instead of its universal application, this method should be used selectively (for example, for high-echelon officials on a relatively defused issue in an organization with stringent entrance requirements). Reasoning and logic fail when, for example, the conditions of the Arrow Paradox (see chapter 2) are met: crudely, a number of people with strongly held but differing preferences.

Misapplication of this method typically results in the desires of the manager who is misusing this control device being frustrated, either through ignorance, misunderstanding, disagreement, or perversity. March and Simon (1958, pp. 129ff.) suggest that when reasoning fails, persuasion, bargaining, and then power politicking are successively attempted.

GOALS

The proper use of goals as control devices is explained in chapter 5 on Management by Objectives (MBO). However, the typical use of goals is to establish quotas, standards, objectives, performance levels, and budgets for subordinates or subordinate units. Often, some attempt to rationalize the goals is made ("the industrial engineering department has determined that the standard time for this operation is 16 minutes"; "your budget has been increased by 3% over last year—in light of inflation and the demands of other units you're lucky to get that much"). Of course, the major precondition for the effectiveness of this control device is the acceptance of the legitimacy of the goal (quota, standard, budget, etc.). At a minimum the authority of the

superior to set the goal (quota, etc.) must be
accepted as being proper; even so, the subordinates may choose to contest the goal overt-
ly (by vocalizing discontent) or, the greater
danger, covertly. The time-and-motion people
(industrial engineers who conduct studies on
the time and motion of blue-collar laborers)
may find they are being lied to. Units may set
very high budget requests, because they expect them to be cut back to the level they
"really" desire. Much of the human relations
literature is filled with cases in which one
party sets an aspiration level on some aspect
of performance for a second party that the
second party deems unacceptable or feels the
action itself is organizationally illegitimate.
Even attributing the goal to a third party
(for example, a respected staff group) will not
influence the perception of an unjust goal.

On the plus side, the use of goals (when the
goals themselves are relatively clear and
precise) can supply clear direction to subordinates, and it is also an effective device
for monitoring the behavior of subordinates
(and effectively supplies coordination—which
I will discuss later on in this chapter). Good
control procedures are those that channel behaviors down desired avenues and those that
permit the organization to determine later if
what was desired in fact occurred. Goals permit
both components of effective organizational
control to be realized, provided that that goal
is operational (see chapter 2 and March and
Simon, 1958). If the goal is interpretable in
any way as being nonoperational and if there
is a dispute about the direction of the behavior or about the degree of accomplishment
of the goal, the dispute will probably be resolved in terms of which party possesses the
greater power.

The preconditions for the use of goals as
control devices are essentially a condensation
of the prerequisites to effective MBO: The
goals must be mutually agreed upon, the goals
must be operational, the behaviors necessary

to achieve the goals must be understood and be feasible, and there must be timely, fair follow-up and evaluation of performance.

It has been noted elsewhere (e.g., Argyris, 1952; Stedry, 1960) what happens when goals, budgets, and so on, are too tight or too loose. In the latter case, there is suboptimal performance and laxness. When demands are too stringent, nonoptimal performance also occurs, but the accompanying feeling of frustration is manifested by different individuals as resignation, apathy, withdrawal, turnover, aggression, and intraorganizational conflict. Ridgway (1956) has noted that even the use of goal accomplishment as an evaluation and control device engenders dysfunctions for the organization.

RULES

A frequent response to a trouble or difficulty by many managers is to generalize the problem, construct a rule to cover it, and apply the rule to the situation. (By "rule," we also mean standard operating procedure—see chapter 4.) This procedure has many apparent advantages: It should eventually treat all significant problems, and the use of rules is "fair" in a crucial way in that it is universally rather than individually applied. However, the probable reason for the preponderant use of rules lies in their externality—managers need not become personally involved in any disputes, they need merely conclude, "Well, I'm sorry but that's the rule, and the rule is law."

Most managers are of two minds about rules, due to an inherent paradox. Managers desire their organizations to be flexible and adaptive, so the organizations can readily follow changing environmental conditions. This argues for few rules and little use of rules. However, as organizations grow larger, their managers wish to retain control over them, and the managers desire uniform and reliable behaviors

by the organization. This argues for more rules
and greater enforcement of them.

Rules, considered as control devices, are
very similar to goals, with two big differences—one being how many rules originate, as
discussed in the previous paragraph, and the
second difference being that there are two
types of rules, prescriptions and proscrip-
tions, that is, "thou shalls" and "thou shall
nots." Basically the requirements for the successful use of rules include clarity, understanding specificity, and acceptance. However,
unlike goals, it is much more difficult to
monitor behavior to ensure that compliance is
being obtained. This is especially true in the
case of proscribed behavior, for example,
"No smoking in this area."

Some authors (e.g., Weber, 1947) envision
the organization's viability as largely resting
upon the use of general, impersonal rules. However, even the Weberian model of organizations
is subject to the same constraints on and
limitations of the use of rules as control devices as is discussed in this section. (The
Weberian theory is a theory of bureaucracies;
a topic which is more thoroughly investigated
in chapter 3 of Mackenzie, 1978. Bureaucracies
rely almost entirely upon rules and authority
as control procedures.)

An aberration that occasionally shows up in
some organizations is to have the reward system
track how well rules are followed. That is,
instead of rewarding the ends that are accomplished, attention is devoted to the rules
(means) employed. The conditions that underlie
this phenomenon are not clear. Apparently
vague, nonoperational goals conjoined with
strong managerial desire for control will suffice.

There is an interesting reaction to the use
of rules (and/or authority) that the recipient
feels is unjust or illegitimate: It is the behavior of "working to rule." To "work to rule"
is to engage in those behaviors, and *only* and
exactly those behaviors, which are sanctioned

by rules and specific orders. Since most organizational tasks necessitate some degree of
discretion, interpretation, and interpolation,
to follow rules and orders exactly to their
letter is to ensure that the organization will
not survive. And who can reprimand a subordinate for faithfully adhering to the rules? A
handful of people "working to rule" can force
even the most secure manager to resign, to be
fired, or to be transferred. It is one of the
most powerful weapons lower-level participants
have in their arsenal for use against their so-
called superiors.

Other weapons available to subordinates are
resignation, absenteeism, strikes, walkouts,
grievances, protests, and complaints through
official organizational channels. The "working
to rule" procedure is usually at least as powerful as any of those other methods and generally invokes a great deal less cost. It is
not clear why the "working to rule" procedure
is not employed more frequently than it is;
it may be due to subordinate ignorance about
its availability, benefits, and costs, or it
may stem from a subordinate's desires to be
flamboyant (e.g., a strike), or vengeful (e.g.,
a complaint to the superior of the subordinate's boss).

In the continuing friction between superiors
and subordinates, the superiors also have a
weapon in their arsenal. They can apply the
rules selectively. That is, "favored" subordinates, for example, those who support the
supervisor politically, are allowed to break
certain rules without penalty (e.g., arrive
late, leave early, not fill out reports). Less
favored subordinates may have the rules selectively enforced in their cases.

POWER AND AUTHORITY

These two concepts are discussed at greater
length elsewhere (Simmons, 1978, chs. 3 and 8),
as is their closely allied brother, supervisory
style (Simmons, 1978, ch. 6), but it is

worthwhile to re-examine them from the perspective of a control device. I interpret the term *power* as being the more general term, subsuming the two more specific terms *authority* (legitimately conferred power) and *influence* (power based upon personal characteristics).

The essential prerequisite for the use of power or authority is the mutual recognition of the imbalance in the distribution of power or the acceptance of its legitimacy (in the case of authority). Many managers recognize that this is the ultimate control device, in the sense that there is no other more forceful control method available, and thus are somewhat reluctant to use it, except when conditions dictate. Such conditions include other control methods having been tried and found to fail, the existence of time pressure or deadlines, large masses of persons to be controlled, persons to be controlled about whom very little is known (e.g., which bars the use of some other control device). In one sense, the conditions are *always* ripe for the use of power and authority. Rules and SOPs are generally created by people who do not have intimate knowledge of the detailed task processes, and if that were not enough, it is noted (see Mackenzie, 1978, for a more complete description and explanation of the authority-task gap) that the rules lag behind changes in the system's processes. So power and authority are needed to obtain the desired changes quickly.

There are several drawbacks to using these ultimate weapons. They may not work; they may not in fact control the behavior as desired, thus lessening the future usefulness of power or authority. Their use personally identifies the manager in the process, possibly increasing his anxiety level, and certainly identifying him with any undesirable outcome that may develop. Since power and authority are never unambiguously endowed on a manager, his power may be contested, and a messy power struggle, which he might well lose, may ensue. Finally, the use of power or authority may in fact

control behavior, but only in the presence of
the authority figure; when the cat's away,
the mice may very well play.

The related control device, supervisory
style, is typically used to refer to the other
component of control, monitoring behavior after
direction has been applied. Several yardsticks
have been employed to analyze and discuss the
effectiveness of various supervisory styles,
for example: (1) close (continuing, frequent
monitoring of progress) and general (infre-
quent, informal checkups on performance); (2)
task-oriented and person-oriented; and (3)
directive and permissive. Some people feel that
person-oriented or group-oriented, general permissive supervisors will be more effective than
close, directive, task-oriented supervisors.
Others feel that another style is "best."
Another style of leadership is to try to be
sensitive to the wishes and needs of one's own
boss and to try to cater to him/her. In short,
one pretty much ignores his own subordinates
except insofar as they merit attention in
order to placate the boss. Still others argue
that the optimal style is contingent upon the
personality predispositions of the manager
and the particulars of the situation with which
he is confronted. My version of the truth is
that we do not yet know enough about the processes by which a manager comes to adopt a
particular style nor the process by which the
effectiveness of that style is determined,
that is, how it is received and interpreted
by his subordinates.

Since people in a group setting are continually adjusting to each other as they learn
more about one another, not only is there *not*
a "best" leadership or supervisory style, but
also all talk of a "contingent" style, that is,
one contingent upon the current situation, is
at best fleeting, since the group context is
changing over time. The process theme will
probably have to be invoked. What is clear,
however, is that an ineffective style usually results in performance inefficiencies and turnover.

The currently oft-discussed control techniques of behavior modification, reward/punishment schemes, and economic incentives are nothing more than particular manifestations of control through power and authority. Any entity that has final say-so over how reinforcers are dispensed (given that the people being controlled desire the rewards and disdain the possible sanctions) has power, and if the reinforcers and legitimacy of the power base are lodged legitimately in the organization, authority exists.

INFLUENCE

Influence is discussed elsewhere (see Kiesler, 1978, who also covers the related topic of conformity), but not from the vantage point of control mechanisms. To influence someone is to use power over that person, but in an informal, nonthreatening way. Instead of ordering someone to do X or setting up a rule requiring that X be done, one says "Oh, by the way, would you mind doing X for me? Thanks very much." Then this influence attempt is either accepted, and X carried out, or it is rebuffed, in which case escalation to a more powerful control device may occur ("I'm not asking you to do X, I'm *telling* you to do X").

The preconditions for the successful use of influence are that one or more of the possible bases of influence is accepted. Such bases include: (1) expertise (if I attribute expertise to person A about subject matter X and if person A apparently uses that expertise to suggest an action to me and I accept his recommendation, I have been influenced by him); (2) charisma (I desire to be thought similar to some admired, high status, reference person or group); (3) reciprocity (I allow myself to be influenced because I expect to be able to influence the other party on some other issue of more importance to me); (4) the desire to be liked and the fear of being disliked; (5) the desire to please.

Rarely are influence attempts directly snubbed; more frequently what occurs is what many managers fear—the slide to Machiavellian tactics. These methods include the following: the request for much advice, but the disregard of most of it; the attempt to form powerful alliances; compromise when it is suitable to one's own ends; the careful release of information, sometimes judiciously withholding it—see Martin and Sims (1956) and Strauss (1962) for examples of these procedures. These procedures are sometimes used to give the appearance of compliance. Some people label such tactics as crafty and deceitful; others view them as being politically astute.

If one can discover a norm of behavior to which a person will conform, whether it is a standard from a professional society, a culturally generated ethic, or an informally group-produced rule (see Group Norms, below), the monitoring phase of the control activity can essentially be dispensed with. The difficulty, of course, is in finding (which is difficult) and producing (which is *much* more difficult) norms for behavior that are both organizationally desirable and evoke conformity.

TRAINING AND HABIT

Probably the most consistently effective control device is training the subordinates so that the desired behaviors become habit (see Simmons, 1978, ch. 5 for a discussion of training). In this way, both components of control are achieved—direction is implicitly supplied by the training, and the need for monitoring vanishes once the trained activities become habitual. The requirements for successful training are essentially three in number. (1) There must be sufficient time available for the training to take place and for the learned behaviors to become habitual. (2) The aim of the training exercise must be reasonably clear and objective, so the trainee can gauge his advancement and so the trainer can know when the exercise is over. (3) The trainee must have sufficient occasion to use his trained behaviors so that they are not forgotten or modified.

Unfortunately, there is a wide variety of factors that mitigate against the success of training and habit. What is learned is not always what is taught. Habits, once acquired, are exceedingly difficult to eliminate or even to modify. If the training occurs in a group setting (as it so often does), informal forces in the group may determine what is learned and the rate at which the learning progresses. It may prove impossible to train those in the upper echelons of the organization, both because of their previously acquired habits and because of their high status and seniority. There are also numbers of tasks and activities that do not readily permit prior training; those that are ill structured, novel, or judgmental in nature, for example.

There is a variety of other training issues for which the available evidence is weak or mixed. For example, does "better" (faster, cheaper, more thorough, more complete, more long lasting, etc.) training result if it is done in-house or through some outside organization? What is the optimal class size? What is the optimal class composition (all from same horizontal slice across the organization, the same vertical slice, or a diagonal slice, etc.)? What is the optimal rate of presentation of information, length of classes, examination rate, and practice time?

WORK NORM GROUPS

Peer group pressure, the felt desire to conform to the norms and standards of behavior of one's own work group, can be a very powerful control device. Peer pressure can dictate what behaviors are acceptable, what activities are proscribed, and the rate, timing, and sequencing of admissible actions. It is very hard to combat the wishes of a unified group of one's own peers. The evidence of this can be seen from the Homans (1950) model of the formation process of group norms. Consider a collection of relative strangers who are organized into a pattern of action that requires that they interact, or consider a similar collection of people engaged in common activities who, through an interaction event, discover their mutual commonality. Necessarily, the people in either collection currently hold, or will hold in the near future, common sentiment patterns (since the same general belief structure is needed in order to engage in a common activity or to be placed in a situation requiring interaction; furthermore, as more interaction transpires, there will be greater pressure to seek resolution of differences). From the common interaction, activity, and sentiment patterns, there will emerge new sentiment patterns (norms) peculiar to this group. Having participated in the formation of the norms, it is very difficult for any of the individuals in the group to ignore the emergent norms and standards.

However, deviancy does occur. Its occurrence is facilitated when the constituency of the group changes or when the required patterns of interactions, activities, and sentiments change. Once a stable group has formed and a new member joins it, the new member is more likely to be a deviant, since he has not participated in the norm formation process. To the extent that any member of the group does not use the group as a referent, the more likely is that person to be a deviant.

There are three other major factors that reduce the usefulness of work group norms as an organizational control device. Probably the biggest difficulty is that most work group norms are not relevant for organizational success; indeed, some are even dysfunctional for the organization. Apparently, management has very little say over which norms are developed and enforced by work groups. Secondly, all

norms and potential norms (e.g., emerging, but
not yet emergent, sentiments) are subject to
screening for legitimacy by the group members.
The less legitimate the norm is perceived to
be, the less control over behavior it exer-
cises. Thirdly, the cohesiveness of the group
also mediates how effectively the group's norms
control its members' behaviors. The more cohesive the group, the more effective are the
norms, and conversely.

Finally, there are a number of relatively
weak control devices that stem from the manner
in which the organization is designed (for more
detail on organizational design issues, see
Pfeffer, 1978; for particular information on
the structural aspects of organizations, see
Mackenzie, 1978). For example, the communication channels that are open to each person exercise some small degree of control over the
organization's behavior, primarily by prohib-
iting some behaviors from occurring and by
facilitating others. As another example, the
amount of centralization/decentralization (relative level within the organization in which
decision-power resides; high—centralized, low--
decentralized) also affects the amount and kind
of control that can be achieved. (A *very* centralized organization admits much rule-use control to the highest levels of management. A
very decentralized organization reduces the
amount of rule-use control available to upper
management, but increases the amount of influence control possible.) Similarly, if the organization is constructed so as to have both
line and staff units (see chapter 8), the locus
of influence expertise will be unequally distributed across the organization.

Other examples of control techniques achiev-
able through organizational design methods
could be presented, but the point is that no
one of these methods by itself yields much, or
even enough, control. When management desires
increased control, it typically does not redesign the organization—instead, it turns to
one of the other control techniques discussed

earlier in this chapter. Infrequently, some
other approach to control is taken. For example, Tannenbaum (1962) reports that increasing
the total amount of control used throughout
an organization is associated with increased
organizational effectiveness. But Tannenbaum is
not referring to control in the top-down, man-
ager-over-subordinate sense used in this chapter. He means reciprocal control, which includes not only the top-down sense but also the
bottom-up sense of workers with influence over
their own situation.

RELATIVELY UNCONTROLLABLE ACTIVITIES

It is a common delusion of managers, though
often unconscious, that all behavior can be
controlled. If necessary, some people are not
unwilling to turn to physical coercion as a
control device. The futility of even that extreme position can be seen from the countless
examples of people willing to sacrifice their
wealth, their careers, even their lives, for
abstractions and principles. If physical coercion cannot completely control behavior, what
chance is there for rules, goals, or influence?
Nevertheless, given reasonable people who have
reasonable demands made upon them, the previously discussed control devices will suffice.
This section will present several normal, frequently occurring organizational activities
that are relatively uncontrollable or at least
not completely controllable (by the previously
discussed devices).

For example, many processes conducted by individual persons are not completely controllable—a person's thoughts, beliefs, and mo-
tives, his pat verbal expressions, his mode of
kinesthetic movement, his private "ways" of
doing things, details in his style of dress,
and so forth. Confronted by the same array of
elemental work tasks, a bewildering variety of
personal styles is used to cope with them.
Some prefer to read their mail first, some to

make telephone calls, others seek a face-to-face meeting, or compose a report, some read memos, some write letters, and some plan the day's activities. Luckily for us all, most managers are usually not concerned with *how* the work gets done, but rather with the philosophy and broad design of the process, that it *does* get done, is done properly, is produced on time, and is within cost constraints. If a manager were perversely concerned with not only the product of the work process but also the minutiae of the work process itself, such a manager would have a very difficult control problem.

Second, many interpersonal processes are relatively uncontrollable. It is known that people have needs for affiliation, belonging, socializing, and reassurance. Thus, informal work groups, friendships, and cliques form. Management has very little say about which informal groupings occur or even that they occur. Management can only recognize that they exist; they should work with them rather than trying to prevent them, minimize their presence, or ignore them. Many organizations operate from the questionable assumption that the less non-task-related interaction among individuals there is, the more efficient the organization will be. Using that assumption, control is exerted to break up the social groupings; degradation in organizational performance is the usual result. Management should also recognize that its workers will interact at various rates at different periods of time. Some workers will seem always to be interacting with their peers; others will seem to be loners. Unless the patterns of interpersonal communication can be objectively shown to interfere with the efficient functioning of the work activities, any management that attempts to control these processes has set a very difficult task for itself.

One very real, important, pragmatic implication of the intrinsic uncontrollability of many personal and interpersonal processes is

the problem organizations have in creating a
physically safe work routine for their workers.
Of course, many organizations do not concern
themselves with creating physically safe work
environments for their employees, and the majority of accidents and injuries occur in such
situations. But even for those humanistic
companies for which worker safety is a concern,
the relatively uncontrollable behaviors of
employees will mean that those organizations
will also suffer accidents and injuries, albeit
at a lower rate than those firms which are not
safety conscious. For example, chemical plants
are necessarily dangerous places to work; no
amount of mechanization can make them 100%
safe. There can be training programs, safety
goals and standards, work rules, and written
communications from the plant manager, but
wearing safety goggles is hot, tiring, and cuts
down on the visual field. Some percentage of
people, in the face of reason, authority, and
common sense, are going to violate safety procedures. Industrial accidents are unethical,
painful, demoralizing, and costly, but many of
them stem from relatively uncontrollable behaviors and thus cannot be prevented.

Third, virtually all extraorganizational behaviors are uncontrollable. Patterns of family
life, recreation, rest, and lifestyle are
largely uncontrollable, yet clearly have impact
on how effective that person is in the work-
place. Contrast the desirability of two workers
who arrive at work on Monday morning: One is
tired, ill, malnourished, hung over, frustrated
and hostile from intrafamily conflict, and the
other is none of those things. Which one will
probably make the more valuable contribution?
What can the organization do about it?

Fourth, organizations are usually unable to
control behavior adequately when ill defined,
novel, and unanticipated events occur. Most organizations do not know what sort of response
they desire to make to major unplanned occur-
rences such as an unfavorable piece of legis-
lation, a major fire or disaster, mass

resignations, or discovery of fraud or other illegal activity on the part of some executives. Since rapid, decisive actions are usually called for in these situations and since the organization does not even know what type of response it desires, the *actual* behaviors taken in those cases are relatively uncontrollable.

To summarize the ramification of this digression, four categories of behavior have been analyzed to demonstrate that there are some organizationally related human behaviors that are not readily controlled by any organization. This point reinforces the usefulness of the process paradigm in analyzing behavior.

METHODS OF ACHIEVING COORDINATION

There are many different reasons why facets of an organization's behavior need to be coordinated. There may be task demands, stemming from the particular characteristics of the organization's structure and its division of labor. It may be necessary to share information to develop more accurate plans for the future, provide a sense of unity and cohesion to individual efforts, permit the relevance of an elemental task to be understood, or supply motivation to units in the organization. Also, coordination may be needed to satisfy people's egoistic needs to feel that they are an important cog, the keystone in which the organization exists.

As is seen in Mackenzie (1978), a need for greater coordination activities among members of a small group implies a degradation in their efficiency. Similarly, organizations attempt to structure themselves so the coordination requirements are minimal. (Of course, there are some organizational tasks that simply require a great amount of coordination—entering a new market, developing international capabilities, changing from manual to computer technology, etc.) It also means that rather simple methods

are employed to achieve coordination, so there
is only a small loss in efficiency. Four such
methods are discussed.

PLANS, SCHEDULES AND DEADLINES

One way of coordinating and integrating the
behaviors of groups and individuals is to establish and adhere to schedules and deadlines,
and to formulate and execute plans. If deadlines are used and if they are common knowledge, then as the deadline time approaches,
people in the organization will know what others are probably doing and can make reasonably
valid inferences about what they themselves
should be doing, in light of both the others'
activities and the activities necessary to complete their own task. In the case in which
schedules and plans are used, the same kinds of
inferences can be made about what desirable
self-activities are, based upon deductions
about where the others are in relation to the
execution of their own schedules and plans.

The desirability of using plans, schedules,
and deadlines is readily seen: Only once is it
necessary to communicate the information to all
parties. Thereafter, there is self-coordination
of the people, with no further communication
needed. To achieve this state, a set of plans,
schedules, or deadlines has to be established,
agreed upon, communicated to all relevant
parties, and understood. None of these four requirements is trivial; none can safely be omit-
ted. Any one of them can take considerable time
to consummate. Lacking that time, perhaps some
other coordination device should be considered.

Besides the failure to establish the necessary conditions for the successful use of
plans, schedules, and deadlines, other forces
may impinge to nullify the usefulness of those
coordination devices. If a deadline or mile-
stone (e.g., from a plan expressed as a PERT
chart) is missed, or if the sequence of activities gets turned around, or if unplanned events
occur (even contingency plans rarely envision

all the strange behaviors that may ensue), coordination based upon plans, schedules, and
deadlines is not going to be achieved. Some
other coordination device is going to have to
be employed, but only after some organizational
problem-solving (see chapter 6) occurs to ex-
tricate the parties from their current morass.

MEETINGS

A second way to coordinate behaviors is to
hold meetings with the parties whose behaviors
are to be coordinated, or to hold meetings with
representatives of those parties and then allow the representatives to hold their own meetings with their own units. (Obviously, this
last procedure can be extended indefinitely.)
Of the two forms (the parties themselves and
representatives of the parties), the former is
vastly preferred, in order to minimize time,
communicate losses, and distortions, and to
maximize involvement. However, simply because
of sheer size, it may only be feasible to have
meetings with the representatives.
Meetings are desirable because of the possibility of *complete*, rather than partial information exchange (e.g., in deadlines, plans,
memos, written notices). Yet, as the number of
participants increases, the subjective sense of
inefficiency grows: The average rate of participation drops, the potential for distraction or
slowdown grows, and social and emotional factors distort the process of information exchange. Of course, holding meetings with representatives only compounds the potential for
problems and errors. Finally, if coordination
problems are so bad as to necessitate meetings,
there is a good chance that more meetings will
also be needed. Meetings tend to breed more
meetings. Enough meetings can interfere with
the accomplishment of task-directed activities.
Probably a good rule of thumb is only to use
meetings as a coordination device when the other devices have failed and when there is time
available to conduct the meeting and any

possible successors to it. Furthermore, it is probably a good policy to try to use meetings to construct some new coordination procedure for the problematic situation.

FEEDBACK AND COMMUNICATION

A third way of coordinating activities is to communicate with the parties involved, or to allow them to communicate with one another. The purpose of the communication, of course, is to permit new information to be fed back into the work activities. That is, the purpose of feedback and communication is to allow all relevant parties to know each other's stage of activity so their behaviors may be coordinated. The communication process may be as informal as an accidental hallway meeting, or more formal, as a telephone call, or extremely formal, as a mandatory monthly report. The coordinative communication processes may be haphazard or they may be forced, depending upon the design of the organization (e.g., which communication channels are open and which are closed, the authority network that reinforces the usage of certain channels). (See Kiesler, 1978, for more information on communication processes.)

The problems with communication or feedback as a coordinative mechanism stem from the occasional inefficiencies with the process and the possible ineffectiveness in getting the job done. To be more specific, the inefficiencies are the occasional times when a great deal of information must be handled, for example, background on the current situation, forms to be filled out and filed, useful information interwoven with extraneous information. Ineffectiveness sometimes occurs, primarily because of misunderstood or error-laden messages; for example, decimal points may appear (when absent) or vanish (when present) either physically or perceptually. The end result is the same—the content of the communication has been garbled. Although it is straightforward to detect and correct "objective" errors (e.g., in the

presence or absence of decimal points), it is
exceedingly difficult to supply the correct
(or even a correct) interpretation to a vague,
semantics-laden message. Terms with unanticipated connotations may be used to convey a
message. In general, communication usage allows information losses, errors, and spurious
information to creep in.

DECOUPLING DEVICES

Since there is no "perfect" coordinative
mechanism (in the sense that it is costless,
guaranteed to work, and applies in all situations), one response to the coordination problem has been to try to obviate, or minimize,
the need for coordination. That is, some efforts have been made to uncouple two or more
units that are interdependent alleviating the
need to coordinate their behaviors. For example, the use of inventories and buffer stocks
is one way to reduce the interdependency between two units. Organizational slack is
another device used to loosen the linkages between units. (Organizational slack may be considered to be the excess manpower employed by
an organization over and above what it minimally requires; see Cyert and March, 1963.) The
presence of slack allows some people to be in
integrative roles and be temporarily assigned
to those parts of the organization that are experiencing coordination problems. Thus, organizations are able to cope with the temporary
absence of persons who are on vacations, ill,
or at conferences. Also, standard operating
procedures (see chapter 4) are constructed
either to have the coordination requirements
programmed into them or to eliminate the need
for coordination. However, since it is not possible in all cases to uncouple or couple
loosely interdependent units, the need for other coordinative devices remains.

OVERVIEW

It is obvious that there is an intimate relation between control and coordination. In the
absence of externally unpredictable factors, a
smoothly functioning and well-coordinated
closed system needs a minimum amount of controlling, and a smoothly functioning and well-
controlled closed system needs a minimum amount
of coordination. To coordinate is to control,
and to control is to coordinate. The real world
is filled with too few examples of smoothly
functioning systems (partly because organizations are open systems with changing external
and internal environments), consequently both
control techniques and coordination devices
are needed. Simmons (1978, ch. 2), in his
analysis of productivity, notes that of the
various factors that affect marginal productivity, ". . . no one input can be changed without
also changing the productive contributions of
other inputs, possibly drastically." Since many
of these changes *do* occur and since their
implications are largely unpredictable by any
single person or small group, control and coordination devices are needed to get the system
"back on the right track." Both types of techniques are needed because in neither case is
there an optimal one. Furthermore, the type
of control device selected affects the choice
of coordination method, and vice versa. A management that controls with goals can coordinate
with plans; one that coordinates with meetings
can control with group norms; SOP use is consistent with control through training and control through rules.

REFERENCES

Argyris, C. *The Impact of Budgets on People*. Ithaca,
N.Y.: The Controllership Foundation, 1952.

Cyert, R. M., and March, J. G. *The Behavioral Theory of the Firm.* Englewood Cliffs, N.J.: Prentice-Hall, 1963.

Etzioni, A. *A Comparative Analysis of Complex Organizations.* Glencoe, Ill.: Free Press, 1961.

Homans, G. C. *The Human Group.* New York: Harcourt, Brace, 1950.

Jabes, J. *Individual Processes in Organizational Behavior.* Arlington Heights, Ill.: AHM Publishing Corporation, 1978.

Kiesler, S. *Interpersonal Processes in Groups and Organizations.* Arlington Heights, Ill.: AHM Publishing Corporation, 1978.

MacKenzie, K. D. *Organizational Structures.* Arlington Heights, Ill.: AHM Publishing Corporation, 1978.

McGregor, D. *The Human Side of Enterprise.* New York: McGraw-Hill, 1960.

March, J. G., and Simon, H. A. *Organizations.* New York: Wiley, 1958.

Martin, N. H., and Sims, J. H. "Power Tactics." *Harvard Business Review* (November-December 1956): 25-29.

Milgram, S. "Some Conditions of Obedience and Disobedience to Authority." *Human Relations 18* (1965): 57-75.

Pfeffer, J. *Organizational Design.* Arlington Heights, Ill.: AHM Publishing Corporation, 1978.

Ridgway, V. F. "Dysfunctional Consequences of Performance Measurements." *Administrative Science Quarterly 1*, no. 2 (September 1956): 240-47.

Simmons, R. E. *Managing Behavioral Processes: Applications of Theory and Research.* Arlington Heights, Ill.: AHM Publishing Corporation, 1978.

Stedry, A. C. *Budget Control and Cost Behavior.* Englewood Cliffs, N.J.: Prentice-Hall, 1960.

Strauss, G. "Tactics of Lateral Relationship." *Administrative Science Quarterly 7*, no. 2 (September 1962): 161-186.

Tannenbaum, A. S. "Control in Organizations: Individual Adjustment and Organizational Performance." *Administrative Science Quarterly 7*, no. 2 (September 1962): 236–257.

Weber, M. *The Theory of Social and Economic Organization.* Oxford, England: Oxford University Press, 1947.

Line-Staff Relationships

DEVELOPMENT OF THE LINE-STAFF CONCEPTS

The concepts of "line" and "staff" originated in classical administrative theory (see Koontz and O'Donnell, 1968; or Dale and Urwick, 1960). Line is concerned with operations, and staff is concerned with support. This dichotomy developed from organizational growth, increased technological complexity, and increased environmental uncertainty. Thus, line managers supervising operations do not have the time, perspective, or resources to cope systematically with the situations confronting them. In response to that, staff units were developed to support, assist, advise, and in general relieve some of the informational burdens of operating line management.

178

However, since stress and conflict typify
the relationship between line and staff units,
this suggests that the taxonomic labels are not
very useful. As we shall see, there are a large
number of organizational roles, some belonging
to an individual person, some to a group or
team, and some to a hierarchical unit, that are
labeled as "staff." For some organizations, the
concepts of line and staff are even reversed.
But the major causes of line-staff conflict are
that the processes of the parties overlap and
their interests and motivations are not har-
monious.

I shall first discuss the design considerations in understanding the structure and behavior of line and staff units; this will consist largely of identifying a variety of staff
roles. Second, I shall investigate the major
causes of line-staff conflict, how the participants react to the conflict, and what may be
done to alleviate it. Third will be an examination of the impact that staff personnel and
staff units have upon the entire organization
when they are considered to be organizational
problem-solving and information-processing
mechanisms.

LINE AND STAFF AS ISSUES
IN ORGANIZATIONAL DESIGN

The broader topic of organizational design is
covered in Pfeffer (1978); nevertheless, some
design considerations will have to be introduced here in order to separate out various
meanings of the terms *line* and *staff*. For example, one factor that influences design is the
nature, type, or purpose of the organization;
consider three such classes--the military,
hospitals, and businesses. The two terms *line*
and *staff* are used differently and have different denotations and connotations in these three
classes of organizations.

Golembiewski's (1961) explication of various
staff roles derives from an analysis of staffs
used by the military. One such role is that of
an aide-de-camp; usually this is an enlisted
person assigned to a high-ranking officer to
assist him in both his professional and cere-
monial duties. Another role is that of the alter ego. In this case another staff individual
works intimately with an officer so as to be
able effectively to double the control that is
possible. For example, when the officer is at
the front, the staff person can continue to
run the office in his absence. There is a support role, for example, logistics or supply,
and there are two advisory roles, specialized
and generalized. The specialized advisory role
is characterized by technical advice givers,
usually located lower in the organization and
usually project directed, as an operations
research group. The generalized advisory role
is typified by the coalescence of generals
from different branches of the military into
one unit to advise the head of the country in
addition to their regular command duties; the
Joint Chiefs of Staff in the United States and
the German General Staff are examples of this
arrangement.

Note from this discussion that the use of
the term "staff" in the military can refer to
a single person (aide-de-camp) or a complex
organization (supply corps); with a great
amount of authority (alter ego), some authority
(specialized advisory), or no authority (aide-
de-camp); whose loyalties are entirely with the
staff role (supply corps) or are only partially
with that role (generalized advisory). The concept of "line" in the military usually just refers to combat units.

In hospitals and related organizations (e.g.,
consulting firms, think tanks, universities),
the term "line" has very little meaning and
usefulness. The main purpose of hospitals is
to cure patients, yet this is done by the
medical "staff." (Similarly in consulting
firms and think tanks, clients receive advice

from the technical "staff;" in universities, the faculty is the "staff.") The hierarchy of administrators (the "line"?) actually provides managerial and clerical support for the "staff." Besides this apparent reversal of roles, the situation is further confused by the presence of actual auxiliary supportive units in a "true" staff role, such as housekeeping, accounting, electronic data processing, and so on. Our vocabulary is not rich enough to permit us to describe adequately this milieu.

Finally, in business firms, line and staff are usually distinguished on the basis of function. Those functions that are central to the survival of the firm are called "line" (e.g., production of goods, sale of those goods), and peripheral functions are called "staff" (e.g., legal, marketing research). However, this arrangement is really misleading. What does one call a labor relations group or the maintenance department? Neither is involved in the production or marketing of goods, yet remove either one and the effectiveness of the firm is seriously curtailed. For that matter, so-called staff groups are occasionally involved in line activities, for example, the legal staff devising a product warranty statement that will become part of the package that a consumer purchases. To make matters even worse, the functional definition of line and staff just will not do, for if even a pure staff group is deleted, it will eventually cause the organization to suffer. Eliminate a pure research department and, although nothing may immediately happen to the organization (except those in high technology, highly competitive environments such as electronics, computers, semiconductors), eventually they will not have competitive products to market.

For all these reasons, it is probably more useful to rank "line" and "staff" on a continuum that measures the degree of centrality of activities to short-run organizational survival. Thus, marketing might be 99% line, maintenance might be 70% line, marketing

research might be 30% line, and research and
development might be 2% line. It would be better if we had more terms to describe ranges
on that continuum (e.g., 1st quartile, "line";
2nd quartile, "support"; 3rd quartile, "staff";
4th quartile, "aid"). However, lacking good
descriptive terms, and for reasons of consistency with the literature, we shall continue to call "staff" any activity that is sufficiently far away from the "line" end of the
continuum.

Even in businesses, staffs play a variety of
roles. Similar to the military, there are
specialized staffs and generalized staffs.
There are two types of general staffs. One is
a suborganization that serves the interests of
the entire organization, for example, a personnel department, data processing, a corpus of
lawyers. The other type is an individual, typically connected to a high-level officer in an
"assistant-to" capacity, for example, the assistant to the plant manager, the assistant to
the vice-president for marketing, the assistant
to the president. Officers sufficiently elevat-
ed in the hierarchy may have a number of generalized staff individuals assigned to them in
an array of capacities, such as a personal
secretary, a chauffeur, an advisor on economic
conditions.

Specialized staffs play one of three types of
roles, or some combination of them; typically
they are also suborganizations, but rather than
serving the entire organization, they serve
some small number of other suborganizations
within the master organization. One such role
is service; for example, the maintenance department serves production, but not accounting,
personnel, or marketing. A second role is that
of advice; a marketing research department
typically only supplies advice to the marketing
group. The third role is that of control; in-
spectors, quality control groups, and cost
control groups typically focus their attention
upon production activities, to the exclusion
of others. It should be well recognized that

there are many specialized staff groups that transcend one narrow role; for example, production control and scheduling provide a service (how to make the manufacturing unit look good) by supplying advice (what they should do) which contains a control element (later progress against the production schedules are measured and evaluated).

Yet another way of distinguishing between, and understanding the nature of, line and staff groups is considering how they fit into the control network. Line groups are typified by the use of legitimate authority; that is, power rests with the office and not the office holder. Authority emanates from the line group in its relations with its own members and with members of other groups, including staff groups (e.g., ordering them to do a study for them). On the other hand, staff groups are characterized by a combination of authority (formal power) and influence (informal power). In some relations with line groups, staff groups exhibit influence (e.g., individual generalized roles, service and advisory specialized roles); in others they use authority—control groups and functional generalized suborganizations often are given authority which supersedes that of line groups. (Furthermore, all staff groups use authority internally to maintain control.) This confusion in types of control (some staff groups using authority internally and influence externally) and the possibility for multiple authority and role conflicts (people in line positions receiving countermanding orders from line superiors and from policing staff groups) contributes to the friction that is so prevalent between line and staff groups.

CONFLICT BETWEEN LINE AND STAFF

CAUSES

The causes of conflict between line and staff groups may be aggregated into three classes:

(1) the differing bases of power for members of the two groups; (2) the different personal characteristics, interests, and motivation; and (3) the procedural linkages. The power ascribed to members of line groups is primarily authority, which is legitimately conferred upon the office (see Weber, 1947). However, other forms of line power stem from seniority (on the job and with the company) and job expertise.

As mentioned before, some staff groups have modest authority over some line operations; for example, cost control, quality control, and safety have the legitimately conferred right to modify production work. The possibility for contradictory commands (overlapping task processes) leads to a natural state of tension between the groups. Although influence, and not authority, characterizes the usual relation between staff and line groups, authority is used *within* the staff group. Occasionally, members of the staff group forget whom they are dealing with and illegitimately attempt to exert authority over members in a line group. The final authority-authority conflict between them emanates from the common dispute over the allocation of scarce resources, typically budget dollars but also including office space, computer time, recognition in the house publication, and so on.

The usual impact that staff personnel have upon line groups is through influence: technical expertise, carefully prepared reports, charisma and charm, academic degrees, political pressure, recommendations of others, possession of vital information and knowledge, and so on. These attempts to influence can be honest and aboveboard, or covert, manipulative, and illegitimate. (The more the influence attempts are rebuffed, the more the means employed tend to slide toward illegitimacy, if the staff group possesses sufficient political power.) Even when some staff advice is accepted and acted upon, other advice must be rejected (and service criticized, and control disputed), else

how can line management publicly remind people
of their proper authority? Even when *most* staff
advice is accepted, line management will have
the sense that the staff group continues to
pressure them with more and more advice, and
thus resentment will ensue.

However, even more dramatic are the attitudes
of the parties which stem from the authority-
influence imbalance when staff advice is offered for use. Line management feels challenged
(to find deficiencies or errors in the advice),
feels superior (due to their authority), feels
more knowledgeable (longer job tenure and more
intimacy with details of job operation), and
also defensive (due to not knowing the technical terms usually present in staff reports).
On the other hand, staff personnel feel frustration (at having their advice rejected or
modified), feel superior (greater technical expertise), feel resentment (at having to work
with ignorant people who probably can't understand the significance of what they are saying), and feel defensive (due to not knowing
all of the details of the job operation and
the details of the history of how it all came
about).

Related to these attitudes are the personality characteristics of line and staff personnel. One distinction between them is their
reference groups and with whom they identify.
Staff personnel tend to be "cosmopolitans";
line people tend to be "locals" (see Gouldner,
1957). That is, the line people tend to side
with the organization, to be seniority-orient-
ed, to favor bureaucratization, and to seek
support and solace from the system of rules.
Staff personnel tend to favor professionalism,
to admire technical competence and education,
and in general to be less loyal to the organization. The impact of this divergence in values
upon possible conflict is obvious.

Dalton (1950), in a study of three industrial
plants, found a number of other differences.
Line managers tend to be older and less educat-
ed than staff personnel. Staff people tend to

be more mobile. The two tend to come from different social backgrounds and have different
recreational preferences. It should be clear
that whenever there are differences between
people or groups of people, the possibility
exists of emphasizing those differences to
stress differentiation, the precursor to conflict.

A third class of factors leading to conflict
is procedural behaviors which characterize the
linkages in and between line and staff groups.
For example, there are usually many more levels
of hierarchy in line groups than in staff
groups. This means that whereas the line managers could be relatively relaxed about the pos-
sbilities for promotion and advancement, staff
managers have to create their own opportunities. Is it any surprise that one group is
labeled "pushy" (the staff trying to get the
line to buy their service, ideas, and advice,
and thus support and advance their cause),
while the other is labeled "passive" or "inert"
(the line trying to select carefully truly useful advice and also to assert their proper
authority)? Also, Dalton (1950) reports that,
occasionally, high-echelon line managers have
a strong say over the promotion of staff personnel. Dalton describes another instance of
"line meddling in staff affairs": Line groups
are occasionally able to force staff groups to
kick back some of their budget funds. The line
groups in this case were able to force this
"deal" by threatening to report to higher-ups
that the staff groups had wasted funds on use-
less, impractical, or unproductive experimenta-
tion and studies. However, staff groups can
sometimes get counter-power over line groups
whenever they fortuitously discover instances
of inefficiency or forbidden behavior —instances which exist in all organizations.

The overlap in task processes between line
and staff groups is inescapable—staff groups
are designed to "interfere" in line operations.
Because line managers are overloaded with responsibilities, they seek to alleviate their

burden by placing some of it on staff groups
(see Mackenzie, 1978, ch. 3 on span of control). But the division between "processes the
line group wants help with" and "processes the
line group wants left alone" is never very
clear. The only way to make that division
clear is to eliminate the staff group altogether so as to fuse staff activities back into
the line roles, and most line managers are unwilling and unable to assume those additional
responsibilities.

There are several particularly dramatic, and
sometimes malevolent, examples of procedural
overlap. One occurs when staff groups develop
endogenous, self-serving goals that drain away
their energies from working on line projects.
In these cases the organization suffers the
worst: It carries the overhead of staff groups,
but line groups receive minimal staff assistance. Another case of insularity occurs when
staff groups have the right to refuse work on
projects. Acting defensively, they may only
choose to accept easy, high-payoff projects.
The reverse case is equally problematical: If
the staff *has* to work on any project assigned
by the line, then the line group can threaten
to assign impossible projects, or projects
with unsatisfiable conditions (e.g., infeasible
deadlines), in order to get the staff to justify pet line projects or to produce answers to
problems that are acceptable to line management. In between these two cases is a situation
that is also unhealthy for the organization as
a whole: The line and staff engage in reciprocity, trading "easy" project assignments for
"right" answers. If the line gets enough power
over staff, they may be able to co-opt the
staff into "yes-men" roles.

EFFECTS

Whatever the causes, line-staff conflict is
viewed (see Dalton, 1950) as one of the four
main causes of intraorganizational conflict,
the other three being: (1) drives to increase

the power of individuals and units; (2) efforts by individuals to increase their status; and (3) union-management disputes. Barrett (1964) reports $50,000 a year being spent annually on *one* conflict between *one* line group and *one* staff group over who was in charge. (The specific case concerned an aircraft overhaul and maintenance base that belatedly created a production planning and control department. Their schedules were not followed. The staff claimed the line was obstructing staff work; the line argued impracticality in the schedules. The facts were that a significant amount of work is discovered *during* the course of aircraft overhaul and maintenance and, because of tight deadlines that have to be met, flexibility in scheduling of work is a virtue. But all the company knew was that it now had a larger payroll and more headaches.) Given that more than a decade has passed since his study, and the size of Barrett's firm, the cost figure he reports is probably neither unusually large nor small.

Seiler (1963) states that conflict can be either exhilerating and motivating, or debilitating and discouraging. It is hard to conceive of a set of circumstances in which line-staff conflict is healthy and functional (except as a stimulus for some higher-level manager to study, understand, and improve that segment of his organization). It usually is costly and dysfunctional. Dutton and Walton (1965), in a field study of two plants from the same company, found that "collaboration" characterized one plant and "conflict" the other. In the plant with conflict, there were some instances of line-staff conflict (e.g., between production control and production), but the researchers' focus was on the conflict between production and sales. Nevertheless, their conclusions about the effects of conflict upon the individuals involved and upon the organization also apply to line-staff conflict. They found that the individuals involved in the conflict suffered great anxiety

and frustration. Professionally, they were
subjected to a great deal of criticism from
their superiors (by contrast, corresponding
individuals in the cooperative plant "com-
mented on their prospects for being moved to
more responsible company positions in the
future"). The effects upon the organization
were a degradation in many aspects of its performance and, apparently, a great slippage in
effectiveness.

Smith (1966) studied the occurrence and effects of intraorganizational conflict in 255
separate units from 6 organizations (36 branch
offices of a national brokerage firm, 4 locals
of an international trade union, 112 local
leagues of the League of Women Voters, 40 geo-
graphically separate agencies of a national
insurance company, 30 separate stations of a
national delivery company, and 33 separate
dealerships of an automotive sales organization). He found that for three of the four
types of business firms he studied (the insurance company, delivery company, and automotive
sales organization), the more conflict there
was, the less effective that firm was; that is,
the less well that firm attained its objectives. In short, for the business firms, conflict interfered with performance.

Another effect of line-staff conflict is how
it alters the behavior of those involved.
Strauss (1962) has conducted an in-depth study
of the ploys used by a purchasing agent in his
relations with lateral departments (and individuals), such as production scheduling,
quality control, and engineering. He reports
five categories of tactics used by purchasing
agents to allow them to forestall conflict,
to cope with actual conflict, and to deal with
the normal pressures placed on them from the
other departments. First are rule-oriented tactics. For example, one procedure is to require
a written justification of a department decision to order some item with a very short
lead time (a practice which causes much trouble
to purchasing agents). This may cause the

department to cancel the request, and it probably makes them hesitant to repeat ordering with short lead times unless absolutely necessary. Another such tactic relies upon their normal behavior which is to ignore using the purchasing manual and other standard operating procedures (e.g., "purchases in excess of X must be put out for competitive bids"). Then, when pressured by other departments, they threaten scrupulous adherence to the rules as a bargaining weapon with the other departments.

The second class of tactics is rule-evading ones. The agent is to comply literally with the request but in an apathetic manner; that is, the purchasing agent "goes through the motions." The passive resistance will placate the department applying the pressure (while meeting the agent's own needs and goals), but not disrupt the agent's relations with outside vendors or jeopardize his standing within the organization. Another rule-evading tactic is to exceed authority, to revise requisitions himself--to extend lead times if he feels production scheduling does not really need to meet the given date, to order in large quantities to take advantage of discounts, to substitute a cheaper brand he feels is equivalent. (This is a dangerous procedure and cannot occur frequently for even the most secure agent.)

The third class is personal-political tactics, for example, the use of friendships to expedite transactions. Sometimes, favors are exchanged. For engineers and managers who are very "reasonable" in their dealings with the agent, he may reciprocate by purchasing personal goods for them at wholesale rates, directing salesmen to take them out to lunch, or being willing to work harder for them when crises develop.

Educational tactics constitute the fourth class. This includes direct persuasion, of course (not to flaunt one's expertise and threaten others, but to educate them), and it also includes manipulation. For example, when the agent finds a cheaper substitute item which

he knows is equivalent, he may use flattery
(of how cost conscious that other department
is) to motivate the department to figure out
how they can use that cheaper product.

The fifth and final class of tactics is or-
ganizational-interactional techniques. The
purchasing agent tries to induce other departments to initiate action themselves rather than
always relying upon him. For example, let the
engineers inquire about available components
before they finalize blueprints; get production
scheduling to ask purchasing what the lead
times on products are *before* they have made commitments. Also, another such tactic is to try
to integrate functions into one department
(his), for example, to try to combine traffic,
stores, inventory control, and production
scheduling into a "materials department" under
his control. The more functions the agent can
assume, the fewer conflicts purchasing will
have.

RESOLUTION

Given the unfortunate prevalence of line-
staff conflict and its serious negative impact
upon many important areas of organizational behavior, what can be done to reduce, mitigate,
and resolve the conflict? Barrett (1964) has
three suggestions. One, keep final decision-
making authority out of the hands of those in
staff positions; that is, try to keep the line-
staff distinction as "pure" as possible. Two,
make the regular career path such that managers
are normally rotated between line and staff
positions. This prevents people from becoming
stale and insular and gives them the perspective of both sides of the situation. Three,
for serious impasses dysfunctional to organizational effectiveness, bring the line and
staff groups together for a frank discussion
of their problems. If such meetings are held
on a regular basis, major problems may never
arise.

Dalton (1950) has six suggestions to offer.

One, create a special body or board charged with overseeing and coordinating line and staff efforts. Two, increase the number of levels of hierarchy in staff groups—but do not increase the number of personnel. (This gives them more advancement possibilities, thus eliminating some of their frustration.) Three, increase the responsibility, but not the authority, of staff officers for the practical working of their projects. Four, require that staff personnel meet some minimum amount of line supervisory experience. Before they are transferred back into the line, you might also require that they have repeatedly collaborated successfully on line-staff projects. Five, top management should take steps to make it clear that they favor neither party, that what they desire is an efficiently running, effective organization. Six, university students (i.e., those about to enter the ranks of line and staff management) should receive more realistic instruction about the social sciences as applied to industrial settings.

As good as all of these suggestions are for coping with line-staff conflict, some amount of conflict between those two groups may be inescapable, for three reasons. First, the structural arrangement between them is always in a state of strain (due to the fact that one side has expertise of a sort but not authority, and the other side has final authority but lacks perspective of an important kind). Secondly, the personality characteristics of the people involved appear to be more consistent within groups and rather different across the two groups. Thus different psychological factors (e.g., different ambitions, different need-satisfiers, different educational experiences) will lead to occasional conflict. Third, the task processes of line and staff managers necessarily overlap (this is necessary so the staff is of some use to the line). The overlap is due to overloading and lack of knowledge, but it results in mistrust and confusion. Properly managing the process overlap is extremely important, as well as extremely difficult. One ultimate possibility would be to eliminate staff groups altogether and to consolidate their functions in line managers, but those people are already largely overburdened with decisions, crises, and information. The line-staff split is useful, as long as the inevitable conflict between them can be held to a manageable level.

STAFF GROUPS AS ORGANIZATIONAL PROBLEM-SOLVING MECHANISMS

In this section we shall address the virtues that staff units have for the organization as a whole. Their primary benefit is to amplify the information-handling and problem-solving capabilities of the organization. This arises just because they are not in line positions; that is, they need not concern themselves with the day-to-day problems and operations (e.g., reorganizing work to account for someone sick or on vacation, meeting work deadlines and quotas, participating on committees, reading and writing reports, supervising subordinates) except to stand back from them and more or less objectively offer comments, suggestions, assistance, criticisms, and evaluations. As noted earlier (chapter 4), day-to-day routine actively shortens one's time horizons and reduces one's perspective; the pressure to get the work done on time is simply too great. By virtue of being free from the day-to-day concerns, staff groups are free from those restrictions. By hiring competent people for those roles, staff units can offer useful advice, assistance, and evaluation to line activities. Three of the information-handling and problem-solving functions of staff groups are important enough to be discussed in some detail: their attention-directing powers, their ability to narrow the loci of search, and their creation of standard operating procedures.

Managers are constantly being bombarded by

stimuli, so many stimuli that "information overload" is a fair description of their situation. Their reaction to this condition is to simplify as much as possible, to heed only exceptional information, to focus upon the work that needs to be done, and to worry about the next upcoming deadline. Staff groups have the time (not to mention the organizational directive) to filter the set of stimuli, to notice patterns and cycles, to detect changes, to note significant and lesser problems. Staff units can direct line attention to significant areas and recurring problems and away from the inessential and spurious. Occasionally, staff units take on some of the problem-solving responsibilities themselves (e.g., an operations research team that develops a mathematical or computer model of some problem area). The result is to give line management a broader spectrum of decision alternatives to choose from and/or a better indication of which alternatives deserve closer scrutiny. For all of these reasons, the attention-directing capabilities of staff groups augments in a significant way the organization's ability to process information and to solve problems.

Staff groups, with their greater time to reflect upon and investigate problems, can also narrow the loci of search for solutions to them. For example, marketing research departments will hold interviews, conduct surveys, perform field studies, and mail out questionnaires to find out what consumers do and don't like about their products or services and to try to find out what they would purchase. The information they glean is used to identify where more intensive searching should be directed. Likewise, quality control, cost control, production control, and so on, all isolate problem areas and in so doing ensure that the search for improvement is not haphazard.

Some firms, having identified a problem area, find that their own staff groups lack sufficient technical expertise (sometimes they just want a second, objective opinion), which often

happens with major, nonrecurring problems. So
they turn to outside staff groups: consultants.
For example, a firm that knows it needs a more
modern computer system may turn to a consultant
for his advice on the three most likely computer system configurations, the cost, installa-
tion time, advantages, and disadvantages. Although this is a novel problem for the firm
employing the consultant, it is a routine problem for the consultant himself (because he does
the same type of study for so many client
firms). The use of consultants to supply advice on problems also narrows the searching
that the firm must do.

Finally, as mentioned in chapter 4, one of
the more dramatic uses of staff abilities is
in the creation and modification of standard
operating procedures (SOPs). The stimuli for
these two events (modification of an SOP and
creation of an SOP) stem from, respectively,
the discovery of a moderate but persistent
change in the decision environment, and in the
discovery of an entirely new decision circum-
stance. That is, firms will occasionally receive feedback that their current set of SOPs
are not working well. In the former case, the
firm will persistently encounter small, negative deviations from what it desires from an
SOP. In the latter case one of three things may
be occurring: (1) The organization recognizes
that it is being confronted by a problem of a
type it has never seen before; (2) an old,
previously successful SOP fails dramatically
and noticeably to a number of people; or (3) a
number of interrelated SOPs may all begin evi-
dencing minor failure. (Should several SOPs begin major failures at the same time, this is
not a problem but a crisis.) In this latter
case, major problem-solving is necessary to
create a new SOP or introduce significant modifications to older ones; in the former case,
adaptation in parameter values for some SOPs
may suffice. But in neither case is the occasion for SOP change likely to be made by
someone in line management (except for crises);

neither are likely to have time to design or alter an SOP and consider, in the design or redesign of it, the impact of the SOP on other parts of the organization's functioning. But staff groups have the time and are usually directed to undertake such activities.

As examples of SOP change and creation, consider the cases of a firm that adds an additional, related product to its product line, and of a firm that develops an entirely new product line. In the former case, minor modifications in purchasing, manufacturing, packaging, inventorying, shipping, and marketing will be needed—not brand new SOPs but elaborations upon the old ones to account for the new product. Much of the SOP change will come from marketing research, engineering, purchasing, cost control, production scheduling, accounting, and so on, probably not by the departments themselves but in an iterated series of meetings with the relevant line groups. In the second case, the same set of actors and functions may be involved, but on a more comprehensive scale. With the new product line, it may be necessary to hire new people with new skills to operate new equipment using a new technology to operate upon new raw materials, and so on. That is, new SOPs are needed. The problems and requirements of inventory, packaging, shipping, marketing, inspecting, and product liability may all be new and different. To create the vastly different SOPs for all of these areas of involvement will necessitate massive use of the relevant staff groups (but the new SOPs will probably be modeled or structured after the old ones).

As I have pointed out, staff units provide service to line groups (e.g., maintenance), advice (marketing research), assistance (purchasing), and control (production scheduling), as well as invaluable information-processing and problem-solving. Although the staff's role and relation to line is often ambiguous, and although tension and conflict epitomize the usual relationship, organizations apparently cannot dispense with the line-staff split, at the risk of being overwhelmed with information, solving the wrong problems, and being unable to adapt to an ever-changing environment, and thus slowly losing their effectiveness.

REFERENCES

Barrett, F. D. "The Staff-Line Dilemma." *Executive* (June 1964): 45-47.

Dale, E., and Urwick, L. F. *Staff in Organization*. New York: McGraw-Hill, 1960.

Dalton, M. "Conflicts Between Staff and Line Managerial Officers." *American Sociological Review* 15, no. 3 (June 1950): 342-357.

Dutton, J. M., and Walton, R. E. "Interdepartmental Conflict and Cooperation: Two Contrasting Studies." *Human Organization* 25, no. 3 (Fall 1965): 207-220.

Golembiewski, R. T. "Toward the New Organization Theories: Some Notes on Staff. *Midwest Journal of Political Science* 5, no. 3 (August 1961): 237-246.

Gouldner, A. W. "Cosmopolitans and Locals: Toward an Analysis of Latent Social Roles." *Administrative Science Quarterly* 2, no. 3 (1957): 281-306.

Koontz, H., and O'Donnell, C. *Principles of Management*. New York: McGraw-Hill, 1968.

Mackenzie, K. D. *Organizational Structures*. Arlington Heights, Ill.: AHM Publishing Corporation, 1978.

Pfeffer, J. *Organizational Design*. Arlington Heights, Ill.: AHM Publishing Corporation, 1978.

Seiler, J. A. "Diagnosing Interdepartmental Conflict." *Harvard Business Review* (September-October 1963).

Smith, C. G. "A Comparative Analysis of Some Conditions and Consequences of Intra-Organizational Conflict." *Administrative Science Quarterly* 10 (March 1966): 504-529.

Strauss, G. A. "Tactics of Lateral Relationship." *Administrative Science Quarterly* 7, no. 2 (September 1962): 161-186.

Weber, M. *The Theory of Social and Economic Organizations*. Oxford, England: Oxford University Press, 1947.

9

Organizational Effectiveness

The effectiveness of an organization is of
concern to all of its participants; an ineffective organization may cause the loss of jobs
for those who work both directly and indirectly
for the organization, may not satisfy the consumers of its goods or services, may cause its
managers to feel frustrated and to lose status,
and may subvert the desires of its owners. The
organization's participants and organizational
scientists want to know what the effectiveness
of an organization is, what factors detract
from being effective, and what may be done to
improve effectiveness. Unfortunately, there is
no consensus on what constitutes an effective
organization, nor on the variables that materi-
ally influence effectiveness. Various writers
seem to favor different interpretations and
define different characteristics of what constitutes an effective organization; this may

merely be an impression they give rather than a true theoretical statement. A brief survey of some of the more well-known approaches is useful.

Probably the term most often used as a synonym for effectiveness is efficiency. (But an effective organization is more than just an efficient one; there are also scattered anecdotes of efficient but ineffective organizations—they behave like clockwork but they do not do anything worthwhile, such as a train that always runs on time but only between two points no one wishes to traverse.) The world of microeconomics is a domain of firms with zero slack, carefully calculating marginal costs and revenues, always behaving rationally and efficiently. One can also find exhortations to efficiency in the scientific management literatures (see, for example, Taylor, 1911), the industrial engineering, time and methods study, management science, operations research, and so on--literatures which are direct descendants of the scientific management thrust. A relatively recent addition to the efficiency field is the emphasis upon automation. For example, Simon (1960) argues that machines will (and should) replace people at those tasks at which the machines enjoy a comparative advantage. I will be discussing particular measures of efficiency (as effectiveness) later in this chapter. Efficiency per se and some of its derivative measures such as profitability and productivity are discussed in Simmons (1978, ch. 2). Also discussed there are the factors and processes which affect productivity, one specific index of efficiency.

A second approach has been to label an organization effective to the extent that it is "healthy." A "healthy" organization is one in which people are satisfied with their jobs, there are few accidents, absenteeism is low (or zero), turnover is low (or zero), and people are loyal to the company. This concern for "health" in the organization first received a significant push from the writings of Mayo

(1945). Lately, the interest is in finding a management or leadership style that promotes health (e.g., McGregor, 1960; or Fiedler, 1967).

In a few instances, for example, Blake and Mouton (1968), concern for people and attention to efficiency receive equal billing in the definition of organizational effectiveness. But rather than including a number of independent dimensions in their definition of effectiveness, most writers focus upon a single dimension, or a tight cluster of interconnected factors.

Yet another approach is to focus upon an organization's flexibility, adaptability, or long-run survival chances (e.g., see Bennis, 1966). That is, organizational effectiveness is posited to be a function of its ability to survive changing environmental conditions. One way to improve adaptability is to adopt nonrigid structures, for example, nonbureaucratic, nonWeberian (1947) ones. Another way is to grow, so there is some "fat" that can be drawn upon in times of crisis. A third way is to work with people individually and in groups and teams so that they do not fear change and so that change, once it occurs, is assimilated felicitously (e.g., see Beckhard, 1969).

Finally, there are those who note that organizational effectiveness is strongly influenced by the degree of "interpersonal competence" (e.g., see Argyris, 1962). That is, to the extent that there is much destructive conflict in an organization, it will be unable to attain its goals effectively. Smith (1966), for example, found several business firms which had diminished effectiveness due to intraorganizational conflict, but, in contradiction, a labor union and a volunteer organization that thrived on conflict.

DEFINITIONS

Having reviewed a variety of the historical approaches to the question of organizational

effectiveness, it is now appropriate to state
and examine more contemporary definitions of
the concept and models of the variables which
influence effectiveness. Before doing so, it
is worthwhile to perform the same type of
analysis on another variable of interest, efficiency, both because of its prior use as a
surrogate for effectiveness and because it is
a significant component of any effectiveness
measure.

Efficiency is usually defined in terms of the
usage that is made of the organization's resources. If all the use that could be extracted
from the resources actually is extracted, then
the organization is 100% efficient. Thompson
(1967, p. 86) defines efficiency as " . . .
whether a given effect [is] produced with
least cost, or, alternatively, whether a given
amount of resources [is] used in a way to
achieve the greatest result." A more operational definition is provided by the open system
theorists, Katz and Kahn (1966): Efficiency is
the output-input ratio of energies usefully
produced and consumed by the organization. (The
motivating analogy they use is that of the
electric motor—how much useful energy is produced divided by the amount of energy consumed.) Input energies to the organization include its capitalization, machinery, raw materials, and personnel. Useful output energies
are the goods and services the organization
exports back to its environment.

Regardless of the definition of efficiency,
attempts to measure it or to determine the efficiency of an actual organization create many
problems. Even if one is willing to measure the
amount of energy by monetary value (which is
probably the best common denominator, but even
so is still a crude one), troubles persist.
Even in the best case, that of a business firm,
there are difficulties in correctly determining
the energetic inputs. (How does one properly
ascertain the value of the personnel's energetic inputs?) For those firms that provide a
service and for nonbusiness firms (hospitals,

governments, universities, labor unions, Girl
Scouts, etc.), it is difficult to construct a
meaningful measure of the energy output.
Furthermore, to employ efficiency measures in
nonfirms can sometimes lead to grave dysfunctions. For example, to make a school look efficient, all that is necessary is to fire a
few teachers to jack up the student-teacher
ratio. The link between efficiency and effectiveness is not well understood.

In spite of these apparent conceptual measurement problems, several efficiency metrics
have been proposed and are in use (but *usually*
just in product-oriented business firms; some
exceptions will be indicated). Productivity is
a familiar efficiency metric, usually con-
sisting of the amount of product manufactured
per direct labor hour, or total labor hour
(direct labor hours are those spent in the
manufacture of products). Sometimes it is recorded as labor costs per dollar of revenue
(this extends it to cover business firms that
supply a service). For some nonprofit organizations, productivity is usually measured in
terms of labor costs per client served. (For
more details, see Simmons, 1978.)

Other efficiency metrics that have been proposed include: (1) wastage per unit amount of
raw material input, (2) rejects per unit output, (3) capital per unit output, (4) idle
machine time, (5) scrap material utilization,
(6) and the relative amount of organizational
slack (which Cyert and March, 1963, define to
be the excess payment to personnel over what
is needed to keep them employed in the organization). The last criterion suffers from measurement difficulties, and the former criteria
only measure partial aspects of what one believes organizational efficiency to be.

Efforts to improve organizational efficiency
are virtually all based upon the misconception
that the organization is merely the sum of its
parts, hence, to improve the efficiency of any
one individual or unit is guaranteed to improve
overall efficiency. Thus, "scientific

management" was aimed at the individual worker, "human relations" at the work group, and "management science" at the function. Suboptimization of the total system is more likely to result from any of these approaches, although they probably will optimize, or at least improve, the efficiency of the isolated system under study. Mackenzie (1978), in studies of small groups, is able to show that the link between efficiency and degree of hierarchy has a correlation coefficient close to one.

An analogous state of confusion and disagreement exists for the concept of organizational effectiveness and for the criteria used to measure it. One common notion is that effectiveness is the degree to which an organization achieves its goal(s) (e.g., see Etzioni, 1964, ch. 2). With this definition, it is relatively straightforward to construct effectiveness criteria. For example, Bennis (1959) proposes that for factories, one should use the amount of products produced; for consulting firms and research organizations, use the number of ideas; for universities and hospitals, use the number of clients leaving; and for service firms and the government, use the extent of the services performed.

However, using goals per se introduces measurement problems ("extent of the services performed"?), intracomparison problems (organizations have multiple goals—how to compare attainment of goal X against attainment of goal Y?), intercomparison problems (how to compare firm A's attainment of goal X against firm B's attainment of goal Y?), and methodological problems (from chapter 2, goals shift over time). Using goal attainment as the effectiveness measure improperly reinforces the values of the goal-creators, usually top management; (that is, to the exclusion of labor and other parties). In attempts to skirt the last argument against the use of goals, Caplow (1959) and Georgopoulos and Tannenbaum (1957) have provided definitions of effectiveness that include the organization's internal

effectiveness as a component. Caplow (1959)
uses a three-part definition of effectiveness:
(1) the performance of required functions, (2)
the minimization of conflict, and (3) the max-
imization of satisfaction. Since with the exception of mathematics it is practically impossible to determine maxima and minima, the
practicability of Caplow's definition is dam-
aged. Georgopoulos and Tannenbaum (1957) avoid
that difficulty, but introduce other problems.
Their definition " . . . subsumes the following
general criteria: (1) productivity, (2) flexibility [successful adjustment to internal
change and successful adaptation to external
change], and (3) absence of intraorganizational strain, tension, and conflict between subgroups." Problems with these criteria
are that flexibility is apparently only
measurable after the fact, and not very operationally at that, and to expect the absence of
strain, and so on, is a bit unrealistic. Smith
(1966) developed empirical measures of effectiveness, for six types of organizations he
studied, "consistent" with the Georgopoulos
and Tannenbaum definition; however, the productivity dimension seems to overshadow the
other two in his metrics. Three examples of his
measures are, first, an insurance company
("productivity records provided by company officials indicating their annual volume of
business"); second, an automotive sales firm
("extent to which actual sales met assigned
sales quotas in each dealership"); and third,
a labor union ("judgments by original researchers of the union's power vis-à-vis their
respective managements").
    If one accepts this definition (of effective-
ness as the degree of goal attainment), then
Price (1968), among others, has studied the
probable (though not yet systematically veri-
fied) determinants of organizational effectiveness. To obtain a high degree of effectiveness,
he argues for a high degree of division of
labor; centralization with respect to tactical
decision-making; an ideology with high degrees

of congruence, priority, and conformity; a high
degree of sanctions; and a high degree of size.
His model stresses that factors in the economic, internal political, external political,
control, and population and ecological systems
all operate upon effectiveness, while being
mediated through the intervening variables of
productivity, conformity, morale, adaptiveness,
and institutionalization.

Mott (1972) has a slightly different perspective on effectiveness, which he defines as
(p. 17) " . . . the ability of an organization
to mobilize its centers of power for action—
production and adaptation." He goes on (p. 19)
to supply three criteria of effectiveness
which are operationalized through questionnaire
items as indicated: productivity (quantity,
quality, efficiency of process), flexibility
(ability to cope with new, unpredicted situations), and adaptability (ability to anticipate
problems, be aware of new solutions, adjust
promptly, and have a large proportion of the
organization adjust).

Mahoney (1967) has taken a completely different tack with respect to developing a definition of effectiveness. He asked 84 managers to
consider 114 variables often indicated as measures of organizational effectiveness. His
factor analytic study of their responses showed
effectiveness reduced to four general dimensions (clusters), which he labeled productivi-
ty-support-utilization, planning, reliability,
and initiative.

The final set of definitions stems from the
system's view of organizations. The closed
system perspective (see Katz and Kahn, 1966)
views an organization as being a self-contained
entity, practically mechanical in its work-
ings. For such systems, their effectiveness
really is the degree to which they achieve
their goal(s). But this is an overly simplis-
tic view of organizations; from chapter 2 you
should recall that the top-level goals of an
organization are rarely operational, usually
shifting, and sometimes in conflict with one

another. By contrast, the open-system perspective views organizations as being dependent
upon and interlinked with many other systems—
governments, suppliers, and consumers to name
just three. Furthermore, the organization itself is made up of a number of interacting
systems, for example, information systems,
work flow systems, and training systems. I will
use the term *focal system* to denote the system
in focus or under study, and the terms *enveloping system* or *enclosing system* or *suprasystem* to denote the larger set of systems that the focal
system is a subsystem of.

The open systems theory definition of effectiveness argues: Since organizations transform resources into products and services,
rather than focusing upon the amount of energy
transported back into the environment and the
desires of top management as to what level of
energy export is good, examine the level of
resources going into the organization. Katz
and Kahn (1966) state this as follows: " . . .
organizational effectiveness [is defined] as
the extent to which all forms of energic return to the organization are maximized" (p.
165). (Since this definition also evokes the
concept of optimization, its pragmatic usefulness is also lessened.) Thus for Katz and Kahn,
overall organizational effectiveness is a function of four components: short-run technical
efficiency, survival power (long-run efficiency, e.g., through improved technology and
growth), profitability, and long-run control
over the entire societal system. However,
Katz and Kahn are careful to point out that effectiveness depends upon one's frame of reference. For example, from the viewpoint of a
monopolist, that organization may be highly
effective. Yet it may evidence reduced effectiveness from the vantage of the societal system (the enclosing system, or suprasystem)—
reduced effectiveness in terms of a restricted
supply of goods at a higher price (than would
otherwise obtain).

Yuchtman and Seashore (1967) drawing heavily

from Katz and Kahn, " . . . define the effectiveness of an organization in terms of its bargaining position, as reflected in the ability of the organization, in either absolute or relative terms, to exploit its environment in the acquisition of scarce and valued resources." They go on to argue " . . . that it is only in the area of competition over scarce and valued resources that the performance of both like and unlike organizations can be assessed and evaluated comparatively" (p. 897). However, they also note that this approach has its own set of problems. One particular problem is selecting a relevant and crucial set of resources on which to assess effectiveness. A second problem is how to handle multidimensional comparisons. Another problem is how to value relatively illiquid resources (e.g., goodwill, reputation, status), and yet another is how to value properly any resource in a rapidly changing environment or in one not characterized by free competition.

The early definitions of effectiveness essentially allowed one to make comparative or relative valuations of effectiveness for similar organizations with similar goals. Later definitions, by including an efficiency component to the definition of effectiveness, allow modest statements of absolute, rather than relative, organizational effectiveness to be made (but only for business firms or others that permit a ready calculation of efficiency). The Yuchtman and Seashore definition " . . . provides the possibility of making accessible for study the large middle range of comparisons involving organizations that have only limited similarities such that they compete with respect to some but not all of their relevant and crucial resources" (p. 902). Still excluded from analysis are organizations that differ markedly in their characteristics, for example, determining the relative effectiveness of prisons and factories.

PROCESS FRAMEWORK

The view of effectiveness adopted here is that it is a quality which can be ascribed to each process in the organization, whether that process is lodged with an individual, a social group, a work group, a separate unit, a suborganization, or whatever. This view is not meant to imply that management should be concerned with or attempt to control all the minutia of each process. Management instead should be concerned with the philosophy behind processes and whether that philosophy is likely to lead to results they desire. Accordingly, each process can be evaluated as to its effectiveness. Then the effectiveness of the entire organization is the *procedural sum* of its constituent processes. (The procedural sum in no way merely corresponds to the usual arithmetic summation such as $2 + 2 = 4$. Since process, when aggregated, simply yield another, albeit more complex, process, *the procedural sum of the effectiveness of two processes is the effectiveness of the resultant process.* The procedural sum may be more, the same, or less than the straight arithmetic sum depending upon whether the two processes aid one another, detract from one another, or have no influence on each other.) Thus it remains to exhibit the procedure for calculating the effectiveness of a unit process.

Processes do not occur in isolation; they are subordinate to an enveloping system. Consequently, *the effectiveness of a process is determined by that larger system.* If the larger system terminates the process, it does so because the process is not effective. If the system continues to feed resources to the process, the process is effective to some degree, the exact degree depending upon the amount of resources fed to the process. (For simplicity and the sake of illustration, presume all the resources used in a process are measurable in some common denominator such as money. Of course, the actual resources returned are multidimensional in character. A difficulty in determining the effectiveness of public, nonprofit organizations is measuring the benefits they supply. Expenditure from and satisfaction with private firms is much more visible.) Then the effectiveness of a process from time period 1 to time period 2 is the ratio of the resources given at the start of time period 2 divided by the resources given at the start of time period 1. (The resources used in these calculations are the equipment, space, material, personnel, etc., necessary to carry out the process. As one moves up the hierarchy, it is necessary to aggregate all of the resources used in processes that are followed by individuals, groups, etc., subordinate to the process under study.)

One may object that this definition of effectiveness may spuriously inflate or deflate the measure of a process's effectiveness due to a general or local change in the level of resources supplied, for example, favorable or unfavorable general economic conditions, start-up of a new unit, phase-out of some untimely operation. The best interpretation of this effectiveness definition is to consider a hypothetical firm that employs MBO (management by objectives—see chapter 5) throughout the entire organization. Then the level of goal accomplishment, whether due to the person's efforts or to exogenous factors, has a strong impact upon his performance appraisal and his subsequent rewarding. Of course, the hope and belief in the use of the MBO system are that spurious events will be highly transient, that a person's own true efforts will show through with a sufficiently long record of his performances. So it is with processes and their resource levels. When a recession or depression hits, all processes in all organizations will probably feel the impact. But if the relative drop in resources for process i in organization j is less than the drop for process i in organization k, then there is good reason to suspect that process i is more effective in *j* than in organization *k*. To use the supra-system's evaluation of a process is the best we can currently achieve in the measurement of organizational effectiveness, even though this currently rates oil companies as being more effective than automobile manufacturers.

The key to this last definition of effectiveness is the return of resources to a process by an enclosing system. To quote from White (1974), the resources returned may be in the form of "skills, knowledge, money, materials, equipment, customers, clients" (p. 367). This properly suggests that decision-making, that is, the allocation of scarce resources, is the central issue before the organization. This concern with resources also allows us to introduce a belated definition concerning the subject of this book: the organization. Again, to quote White (1974, p. 367), an organization is a "formally constituted collectivity which utilizes resources." Finally, the emphasis on resource return allows an interesting analogy to be drawn. Observe the dualism between the concepts of effective organizations getting the most resources returned to them and Darwin's evolutionary theory in which organisms that are the fittest survive; that is, those able to extract and make best use of the resources available in their current environmental situation. The analogy should probably not be pushed too hard, but it does suggest that those organizations willing and able to evolve and change are the ones most likely to persist.

PARTIALLY DETERMINING FACTORS

Now that we have reviewed the state of definitions of organizational effectiveness in order to appreciate other viewpoints and to see the apparent superiority of the process approach, we need to see what kind of theory of effectiveness can be constructed using the last definition. That is, what levers does a manager manipulate in order to increase his

organization's effectiveness? Of course, no
definitive theory yet exists; all we can discuss are some factors which, taken together,
are thought to affect the level of a system's
effectiveness. Three characteristics of the
focal system will be examined (efficiency,
internal integration, and rigidity), and three
characteristics of the enclosing suprasystem
will be examined (environmental munificence,
coordination requirements, and required task
process changes). After introducing these six
characteristics, we shall discuss how some of
the interactions between them influence effectiveness.

The efficiency of a process during a time period re-
fers to the proportion of consumed resources that is ex-
ported as useful energy. Resources that are typically *not* consumed during a time period are
land, equipment, and buildings. Materials,
personnel time, and actual physical deprecia-
tion to "long-term" assets are common resources that are consumed. "Useful energy" refers to goods or services that the larger system values and can put to use. (Of course, the
suprasystem may neglect in the short-run to
value properly all resources consumed and
services returned, such as clean air, unpol-
luted streams, energy stockpile.) Obviously,
a process is going to have to be somewhat efficient in order to be effective. If its efficiency is very low or zero, the enclosing
system is feeding it many resources and getting
very little in return; it might as well terminate the process. On the other hand, increasing
efficiency is no guarantee that effectiveness
will be improved. Imagine a process that is 80%
efficient and yields an amount of energy to its
larger system; suppose now its efficiency rises
to 90% and that now an amount $m + \Delta m$ of energy
is transported to the enclosing system. This
may or may not increase the effectiveness of
this process; it will if the larger system can
make use of the additional amount Δm of energy.
But if the enveloping system can only use the
amount m of energy, then the Δm amount is

wasted and the process is no more effective. A "worst case" analysis indicates that the new amount Δm of energy may actually cause a *reduction* in effectiveness if other resources must be diverted to inventory, package, count, test, ship, and so on, the new amount Δm of energy. (Of course, if the system can redesign itself to make use of the new amount Δm of energy, then increased effectiveness will result. But that takes time, and for the short run, the basic argument holds.)

Thus the relationship between efficiency and effectiveness is not as simple as one might naively expect. It is true that over a wide range of efficiency (for illustration purposes only, possibly between 15% and 85%), the relationship is direct—increase efficiency and effectiveness increases. At the lower end (0-15% efficiency). one expects there to be no relationship (increase efficiency and get no improvement in effectiveness). and at the upper ranges of efficiency (85-100%), it may well be an inverse relation (increase efficiency and reduce effectiveness). But lacking careful empirical investigation, we can only admit the possibility that no one of the three forms of relationship (direct, inverse, and none) is logically prohibited from holding between efficiency and effectiveness.

Internal integration only refers to the subprocesses of the focal process, specifically, whether they cooperate or compete, whether the persons who execute the processes share values, attitudes, and so on, and whether the processes are reliable (i.e., they make consistent, predictable demands upon resources, cycle through a consistent, predictable length of time, and result in a consistent, predictable amount and mix of output). Some organizational tasks (e.g., manufacturing) require highly internally integrated processes. The degree of internal integration has very little effect on other tasks, such as research. And the level of accomplishment of some organizations is predicated upon processes that are not internally integrated. For example, labor unions are

generally most effective when there is strife
and tension in the parent organization.

*Rigidity denotes the nonexistence of metaprocesses to
change other processes (or introduce new processes) to
track dynamic conditions.* Some organizational tasks
are characterized by rapid change (e.g., anything employing computer software); others
exhibit no measurable change over long stretches of time (e.g., retail selling of clothes).
Rigid processes used to accomplish a dynamic
task will only be effective in the short-run,
but rigid processes for stable tasks permit
effectiveness to be obtained.

*Environmental munificence refers to the relative re-
source "richness" of the enveloping system for the process under study.* Relatively rich systems can reward processes that would not otherwise be effective, and relatively impoverished systems
cannot reward otherwise effective processes
that merit it. There is no guarantee of justice
in the universe as we know it.

*Coordination requirements refers to the degree to
which the enclosing environment requires coordinated efforts to extract resources from it.* Some suprasys-
tems, for example, the military or the production of consumer appliances, require much coordination. Others, such as retail sales and
the production of art, necessitate relatively
little coordination. In a sense, coordination
requirements refers to task complexity, but as
Simon (1962) points out, there are several
ways of lessening complexity and required coordination (e.g., factor into nearly decompos-
ible subsystems, organize into a hierarchy).

*The required task process changes means the extent to
which the suprasystem's technology, marketplace, personnel, and so on, are changing.* With these or similar
changes occurring in the system's environment,
the previously employed set of task processes
no longer suffices to extract resources from
the environment at the same rate. In order to
continue garnering resources at the same rate,
the task processes have to be changed.

First consider the separate effects of these
six factors. Holding the three suprasystem

characteristics at a constant level, one way to increase a system's effectiveness is to improve its three input characteristics (with the nuances as previously discussed). Alternatively, if the system itself is unwilling or unable to change in order to improve its own effectiveness, it should seek out a suprasystem with preferred characteristics.

In addition to these factors separately influencing effectiveness, there are also important interactions among them. Only *some* of the two-factor interactions are next described; the remaining two- three- and four-factor interactions await a more careful specification of the theory.

Environmental munificence probably amplifies or retards the effects of the other factors. For example, if the system is rigid, yet conditions change quickly, and the system's environment is relatively resource-poor, that system's effectiveness will rapidly approach zero. Yet given the same system in a resource-rich environment, it will probably continue to be effective. Happily, most systems exist in environments that are neither abundant nor deficient in resources (i.e., effort is required to bring them forth, and they are available), so the rigidity characteristic can run its usual course.

The relationship between effectiveness and internal integration is that the level of internal integration acts as a barrier against changes in effectiveness; however, whether that barrier is a "floor" or a "ceiling" depends upon other conditions. For systems that have high coordination requirements (e.g., manufacturing), the level of internal integration places a ceiling upon effectiveness—if that level of internal integration should drop, so will effectiveness. For those systems that are most effective when the requirements are low (e.g., labor unions), it probably acts as a floor—reduce the level of internal integration and effectiveness actually increases. Internal integration and coordination requirements affect efficiency analogously, which in turn amplifies the effects on effectiveness.

The level of environmental munificence can inflate or deflate the degree of internal integration and its importance for determining effectiveness. In times of plenty, interpersonal differences tend to be viewed as minor and unimportant, but in times of scarcity, even slight differences are exaggerated. In spite of this amplification, the level of environmental munificence, once it strays out of a broad middle range, is probably a more important factor in determining effectiveness than is the degree of internal integration.

Before going on to examine a few empirical studies of effectiveness, the reader should be reminded that we have only been discussing several of the many factors that influence effectiveness and that these factors only partially determine the degree of effectiveness. This is necessarily a preliminary statement of hypothesized relationships.

EMPIRICAL STUDIES

There have been few empirical studies of organizational effectiveness for a number of good reasons. A good definition of organizational effectiveness has been lacking. In fact to conduct a careful, longitudinal empirical study would require massive amounts of data collection, manipulation, and interpretation. Also, Likert (1958) has reasoned that there are inadequate measurements of many important variables of organizational performance. In spite of these difficulties, there are a few studies that can be considered here.

One such class of studies is the work being done on MBO (see chapter 5 of this book and remember all of the qualifications upon the MBO process that I detailed there). MBO is the process of having each and every superior-subordinate pair periodically meet to negotiate operational goals to guide the

subordinate's behaviors through the next time
period, and to review and assess his performance during the previous time period against
the goals developed for it. A number of MBO
field studies (see chapter 5) have demonstrated the utility of MBO for improving attitudes, productivity, commitment, and the
level of goal accomplishment. Although MBO has
not been tested for its impact upon organizational effectiveness as that term is defined
in this chapter, the signs are present that
MBO affects it favorably.

MBO is probably successful at improving
organizational effectiveness because it promotes internal integration, favors efficiency,
combats rigidity, and continually calls into
reexamination at all layers and levels the
goals and activities of the system; that is,
searching occurs for methods to earn greater
resource return. Internal integration is
heightened thanks to the requirement that each
and all superior-subordinate dyads mutually
agree on the subordinate's goals and activities
for the ensuing time period. Periodic evaluation and assessment of performance favors efficient operations. Of course, the periodic
performance review and redirection of efforts
lessens the chances for rigidity. Thus the
theory of organizational effectiveness sup-
ports the contention that the proper use of
MBO will improve effectiveness.

Smith (1966) studied 250 separate organizational units from 6 organizations (union,
League of Women Voters, delivery firm, automotive sales organization, insurance company,
brokerage firm) to investigate some causes of
intraorganizational conflict and its effect
upon organizational effectiveness. He hypothesized that the conflict could be attributed to
communication problems, differences in interests and goals, and dissimilar attitudes or
perceptions. His findings were that the three
hypothesized causes of intraorganizational conflict were ". . . more appropriate to the
business organizations than to the union or the

voluntary organization" (p. 518). He also
found that intraorganizational conflict had
negative consequences for the four business
firms, but it was beneficial for the union and
the voluntary organization. These results are
entirely consistent with the theory of the
effects of internal integration on organizational effectiveness.

Georgopoulos and Tannenbaum (1957) studied
"an industrial service specializing in the
delivery of retail merchandise" (p. 535). They
were interested in considering the relationship between three variables (organizational
productivity, flexibility, and strain) and organizational effectiveness, which they define
". . . as the extent to which an organization
as a social system, given certain resources
and means, fulfills its objectives without in-
capacitating its means and resources and without placing undue strain upon its members"
(p. 535). By examining 32 "stations" (a subunit of the division which is the major unit
of a company plant—a typical station had 3
supervisors and 35 workers), they found that
station productivity and flexibility fostered
station effectiveness and that intergroup
strain retarded station effectiveness. These
results are completely consistent with the
previously presented theory of organizational
effectiveness. They also found considerable
intercorrelations among the three variables:
Intergroup strain was negatively correlated
with productivity and flexibility, and productivity and flexibility were positively correlated with each other. This too is consistent
with previous discussions.

Similar to Mahoney (1967), Webb (1974) performed a factor analytic study of the organizational characteristics that promote effectiveness in churches, for which he defined
effectiveness as the degree of goal attainment.
He identifies four clusters as being the most
important contributors. They are cohesion
(team spirit—to use our term, *internal integration*), efficiency (little wastage), adaptability

(the congregation's readiness to accept change —the reverse of rigidity), and support (the degree to which the membership stands behind the minister—environmental munificence).

Rushing (1974) studied profit and nonprofit hospitals. Using Thompson's (1967) efficiency measure, he found significant differences between them. Using Yuchtman and Seashore's (1967) definition of effectiveness (ability of a hospital to exploit its community's resources by charging more), he found that profit-making hospitals were more effective than their nonprofit counterparts even though the profit-making hospitals were not as efficient. (The nonprofit hospitals were probably forced into greater efficiency by trying to supply the same level of services but with a lesser resource base to work from.)

Thus, the little empirical work that has been reported suggests the theory of organizational effectiveness presented in this chapter. But before one can have much faith in that theory, more work, both theoretical and empirical, will have to be performed. Sadly, that same statement can be applied to *any* extant theory in the field of organizational science. You may view this state of affairs as some combination of the following: Good reason for not believing any of it, good reason for applying organizational theories cautiously, and opportunities for ambitious people.

REFERENCES

Argyris, C. *Interpersonal Competence and Organizational Effectiveness*. Homewood, Ill.: Dorsey, 1962.

Beckhard, R. *Organizational Development: Strategies and Models*. Reading, Mass.: Addison-Wesley, 1969.

Bennis, W. G. "Leadership Theory and Administrative Behavior: The Problem of Authority. *Administrative Science Quarterly* 4, no. 3 (December 1959): 259-301.

Bennis, W. G. *Changing Organizations*. New York: McGraw-Hill, 1966.

Blake, R. R., and Mouton, J. S. *Corporate Excellence through Grid Organization Development*. Houston, Texas: Gulf, 1968.

Caplow, T. "The Criteria of Organizational Success." In *Readings in Human Relations*, edited by K. Davis and W. G. Scott. New York: McGraw-Hill, 1959.

Cyert, R. M., and March, J. G. *A Behavioral Theory of the Firm*. Englewood Cliffs, N.J.: Prentice-Hall, 1963.

Etzioni, A. *Modern Organizations*. Englewood Cliffs, N.J.: Prentice-Hall, 1964.

Fiedler, F. E. *A Theory of Leadership Effectiveness*. New York: McGraw-Hill, 1967.

Georgopoulos, B. S., and Tannenbaum, A. S. "A Study of Organizational Effectiveness." *American Sociological Review* 22 (1957): 534-540.

Katz, D., and Kahn, R. L. *The Social Psychology of Organizations*. New York: Wiley, 1966.

Likert, R. "Measuring Organizational Performance." *Harvard Business Review* (March-April 1958).

Mackenzie, K. D. *Organizational Structures*. Arlington Heights, Ill.: AHM Publishing Corporation, 1978.

Mahoney, T. A. "Managerial Perceptions of Organizational Effectiveness." *Management Science* 14, no. 2 (October 1967): B76-B91.

Mayo, E. *The Social Problems of an Industrial Civilization*. Boston, Mass.: Division of Research, Harvard Graduate School of B. Admin., 1945.

McGregor, D. *The Human Side of Enterprise*. New York: McGraw-Hill, 1960.

Mott, P. E. *The Characteristics of Effective Organizations*. New York: Harper and Row, 1972.

Price, J. L. *Organizational Effectiveness: An Inventory of Propositions*. Homewood, Ill.: Irwin, 1968.

Rushing, W. "Differences in Profit and Nonprofit Organizations: A Study of Effectiveness and Efficiency in General Short-Stay Hospitals." *Administrative Science Quarterly* 19, no. 4 (December 1974): 474-484.

Simmons, R. E. *Managing Behavioral Processes: Applications of Theory and Research.* Arlington Heights, Ill.: AHM Publishing Corporation, 1978.

Simon, H. A. "The Corporation: Will It Be Managed by Machines?" In *Management and Corporations 1985,* edited by M. Anshen and G. L. Bach. New York: McGraw-Hill, (1960): 17–55.

Simon, H. A. "The Architecture of Complexity." *Proceedings of the American Philosophical Society 106,* no. 6 (December 1962): 467–482.

Smith, C. "A Comparative Analysis of Some Conditions and Consequences of Intra-Organizational Conflict." *Administrative Science Quarterly* 10 (March 1966): 504–529.

Taylor, F. W. *The Principles of Scientific Management.* New York: Harper, 1911.

Thompson, J. D. *Organizations in Action.* New York: McGraw-Hill, 1967.

Webb, R. J. "Organizational Effectiveness and the Voluntary Organization." *Academy of Management Journal* 17, no. 4 (December 1974): 663–677.

Weber, M. *The Theory of Social and Economic Organization.* Oxford, England: Oxford University Press, 1947.

White, P. E. "Resources as Determinants of Organizational Behavior." *Administrative Science Quarterly* 19, no. 3 (September 1974): 366–379.

Yuchtman, E., and Seashore, S. E. "A System Resource Approach to Organizational Effectiveness." *American Sociological Review* 32, no. 6 (December 1967): 891–903.

Name Index

Adams, J. S., 53, 72
Adams, S., 141, 142, 148
Anderson, B., 142, 143, 149
Argyris, C., 34, 49, 157, 175, 201, 219
Arrow, K., 36, 37, 46, 155

Barrett, F. D., 188, 191, 197
Beckhard, R., 201, 219
Bennis, W. G., 35, 49, 201, 204, 219
Berlew, D. E., 49
Berry, P. C., 131, 149
Blake, R. R., 201, 220
Blau, P. M., 131, 148
Block, C. H., 131, 149
Blood, M. R., 105, 124

Braybrooke, D., 27, 45, 46, 48, 49, 129, 138, 148

Caplow, T., 54, 55, 72, 204, 205, 220
Carroll, S. J., 109, 117, 120, 121, 123
Carter, E. E., 137, 138, 148
Chertkoff, J. M., 57, 58, 67, 72, 73
Clarkson, G. P. E., 13, 21, 87, 96, 97, 99, 101
Cohen, M. D., 27, 49, 79, 101, 139, 149
Crecine, J. P., 99, 101
Cummings, L. L., 130, 149
Cyert, R. M., 13, 22, 29, 39, 40, 42, 45, 48, 49, 88, 89, 100, 102, 132,

134, 149, 174, 176,
203, 220

Dale, E., 178, 197
Dalton, M., 185, 186,
187, 191, 197
Davis, O. A., 101, 102
Dearborn, D. C., 135, 149
Delbecq, A. L., 130, 149
Dickson, W. J., 71, 73
Drucker, P., 105, 109,
123
Dutton, J. M., 188, 197

Eilon, S., 84, 102
England, G. W., 26, 49
Etzel, M. J., 120, 123
Etzioni, A., 60, 72, 153,
176, 204, 220

Fiedler, F. E., 201, 220
Forrester, J. W., 14, 22
French, J. R. P., 120, 124

Gamson, W. A., 56, 72
Georgiou, P., 45, 48, 49
Georgopoulos, B. S., 204,
205, 218, 220
Gergen, K. J., 53, 72
Gerwin, D., 99, 102
Golembiewski, R. T., 180,
197
Gouldner, A. W., 185, 197
Gregg, L. W., 13, 15, 22
Gumpert, P., 60, 72

Heller, J., 89, 102
Hempel, C. G., 11, 12, 13,
22
Homans, G. C., 53, 72,
165, 176
House, R. J., 111, 124
Howard, J. A., 101, 102

Hulin, C. L., 105, 124
Hyman, R., 142, 143, 149

Ivancevich, J. M., 117,
120, 122, 123, 124

Jabes, J., 45, 49, 71, 72,
75, 93, 101, 135, 149,
153, 176

Kahn, R. L., 202, 206, 207,
208, 220

Katz, D., 202, 206, 207,
208, 220
Kay, E., 120, 124
Kelley, H. H., 53, 73
Kepner, C. H., 143, 145,
146, 149
Kiesler, S., 53, 68, 73,
75, 93, 102, 162, 173,
176
Komorita, S. S., 57, 58,
67, 73
Koontz, H., 178, 197
Kuhn, T. S., 7, 22

Levinson, H., 115, 124
Likert, R., 105, 124, 216,
220
Lindblom, C. E., 27, 45,
46, 48, 49, 129, 138,
148
Luce, R. D., 36, 49, 57,
73

Mackenzie, K. D., 4, 22,
44, 49, 70, 73, 158,
160, 166, 170, 176, 187,
197, 204, 220
Mahoney, T. A., 206, 218,
220
March, J. G., 13, 22, 27,

29, 32, 35, 39, 40, 42,
45, 48, 49, 66, 73, 78,
79, 85, 88, 89, 100,
101, 102, 131, 132,
134, 139, 149, 150,
155, 156, 174, 176,
203, 220
Markowitz, H., 96, 102
Martin, N. H., 163, 176
Mayo, E., 200, 220
McGregor, D., 105, 124,
153, 176, 201, 220
Meyer, H. H., 120, 124
Milgram, S., 151, 176
Mintzberg, H., 47, 48,
49
Morgenroth, W. M., 101,
102
Morse, N. C., 105, 124
Mott, P. E., 206, 220
Mouton, J. S., 201, 220

Odiorne, G., 107, 109,
119, 124
O'Donnell, C., 178, 197
Olsen, J. P., 27, 49, 79,
101, 139, 149
Osborn, A. F., 131, 149

Perrow, C., 30, 38, 49
Peters, G., 101, 103
Pfeffer, J., 44, 50, 70,
73, 95, 102, 111, 124,
150, 166, 176, 179,
197
Popper, K. R., 10, 22
Portugal, S. H., 132, 149
Pounds, W. F., 109, 124,
129
Price, J. L., 205, 220

Rados, D. L., 101, 102
Raia, A. P., 109, 120,
121, 124
Raiffa, H., 36, 50, 57, 73

Reimer, E., 105, 124
Ridgway, V. F., 104, 124,
157, 176
Roethlisberger, F., 71, 73
Rotter, G. S., 132, 149
Rueter, F. H., 101, 102
Rushing, W., 219, 220

Schein, E. H., 49
Scott, W. R., 131, 148
Seashore, S. E., 207, 208,
219, 221
Seiler, J. A., 34, 50, 188,
197
Shapley, L. S., 56, 57, 73
Sherif, M., 35, 50
Shubik, M., 56, 57, 73
Shull, F. A., 130, 149
Simmons, R. E., 54, 71, 73,
93, 102, 159, 163, 175,
176, 200, 203, 221
Simon, H. A., 13, 15, 22,
26, 27, 32, 35, 49, 50,
66, 73, 76, 78, 85, 102,
131, 132, 135, 138, 149,
150, 155, 156, 176, 200,
214, 221
Sims, J. H., 163, 176
Skinner, B. F., 8, 22
Smith, C. G., 189, 197,
201, 205, 217, 221
Smith, W., 60, 72
Solzhenitsyn, A. I., 99,
100, 102
Stedey, A. C., 157, 176
Steele, F. I., 49
Strauss, G. A., 163, 176,
189, 197
Swinth, R. L., 146, 147,
149

Tannenbaum, A. S., 167,
176, 204, 205, 218,
220
Taylor, D. W., 131, 149

Taylor, F. W., 200, 221
Thibaut, J. W., 53, 73
Thompson, J. D., 30, 47,
    50, 79, 102, 103, 202,
    219, 221
Tichy, N., 59, 60, 73
Tosi, H. L., 109, 117,
    120, 121, 123
Trego, B. B., 143, 145,
    146, 149
Tuden, A., 79, 102

Urwick, L. F., 178, 197

Varney, G. H., 115,
    124

Walton, R. E., 188,
    197
Webb, R. J., 218, 221
Weber, C. E., 101, 103
Weber, M., 158, 177, 184,
    198, 201, 221
White, P. E., 211, 221

Yuchtman, E., 207, 208,
    219, 221

Subject Index

Adaptability (Organizational), 201
Aspiration-Level Theory, 29, 30
Attribute-Value Pair, definition of, 3
Authority as a Method of Control, 159

Bargaining, Theories of, 54
Bounded Rationality, 76

Cabal, 19, 52
Cabal, definition of, 52
Clique, 19, 40, 52
Clique, definition of, 52
Coalition, 19, 40, 52

Coalition, definition of, 52
Coalition, Theories of Formation, 52
Communication as a Method of Coordination, 173
Completeness, definition of, 11
Conflict, Analyzed through knowledge of Organizational Goals, 34
Conflict, Between Line and Staff Units, 183
Conflict, Quasi-Resolution of, 135
Conflict Resolution Processes, 35, 191
Control, 20, 182
Control, Activities One is Unable to, 167
Control, Methods of

Achieving, 154
Control, Uses of, 150
Control Problems with
  Standard Operating
  Procedures (SOPs), 94
Coordination, 20, 150,
  170
Coordination, Methods
  of Achieving, 170
Coordination, Uses of,
  150
Coordination Require-
  ments, their Effects
  upon Effectiveness,
  214
Cosmopolitan - Local, 185
Cumulative Theory, defini-
  tion of, 16

Deadlines as a Method of
  Coordination, 171
Decision Making, Norma-
  tive, 142
Decision Problem, defini-
  tion of, 75
Decision Procedures, SOPs
  Considered as, 82
Decision Processes in use
  by a Coalition, 70
Decisional Uses of Goals,
  25, 26
Decisions, Constrained
  Optimizing, 86
Decisions, Optimizing, 85
Decisions, Satisficing,
  85
Decoupling Devices as a
  Method of Coordination,
  174
Deductive-Nomological
  Reasoning, definition
  of, 12
Descriptive Uses of Organi-
  zational Goals, 28

Discriminative Nets, 83
Dominant Coalition, def-
  inition of, 39

Effectiveness, defined
  from System's Per-
  spective, 207, 208
Effectiveness, defined in
  terms of Goal Ac-
  complishment, 204
Effectiveness, defined in
  terms of Processes,
  209
Effectiveness, Organiza-
  tional, 104, 199, 204
Efficiency, definition of,
  202, 203, 212
Efficiency, its Effects
  upon Effectiveness,
  212
Efficiency, Organization-
  al, 71, 120, 168, 199,
  202, 203, 212
Elegance, definition of,
  12
Environmental Munificence,
  its Effects upon Ef-
  fectiveness, 214
Evaluation System, 70,
  105, 106, 107, 152,
  158
Exchange, Theories of Be-
  havior, 53
Exhortative Uses of Or-
  ganizational Goals, 31

Face Validity, definition
  of, 12
Feedback as a Method of
  Coordination, 173
Flexibility (Organization-
  al), 201
Formal Groups (*See* In-
  formal Groups)

Free Will Paradigm, definition of, 7

Generality, definition of, 10
Goal, 18, 23, 24, 106, 121, 122, 151, 152, 155
Goal, Decisional Uses of, 25, 26
Goal, Descriptive Uses of, 25, 28
Goal, Devices for Stabilizing, 42, 110
Goal, Exhortative Uses of, 25, 31
Goal, Official, definition of, 30
Goal, Operational, 35
Goal, Operative, definition of, 30
Goal, Superordinate, 35
Goal, Uses to Analyze Conflict, 25, 34
Goal Formation, 36
Goal Paradigm, Counterarguments to, 45
Goals as a Method of Control, 155
Goals as affected by Informal Groups, 67
Goals, Considered as Measures of Organizational Effectiveness, 204

Habit, as a Method of Control, 163
Health, Organizational, 200
History (of a system), definition of, 3

Influence as a Method of Control, 162

Informal Groups, definition of (and distinguished from Formal Groups), 52
Informal Groups, their Effects upon Goals, 67
Informal Groups, Theories of Formation of, 52
Internal Integration, its Effects upon Effectiveness, 213

Line-Staff, 21, 144, 178
Line-Staff, Various Roles of, 179, 180
Line-Staff Conflict, Causes of, 183
Line-Staff Conflict, Resolution of, 191
Local-Cosmopolitan (*See* Cosmopolitan-Local)
Logic, as a Method of Control, 154

Management by Exception, 108
Management by Objectives (MBO), 20, 44, 104, 155, 217
MBO, Implementation of, 113
MBO, Philosophy of, 106
MBO, Theory of, 111
MBO considered as a procedure for improving Effectiveness, 217
Management, Participative, 105
Meetings as a Method of Coordination, 172

Norms, Work Group, 53
Norms, Work Group, as a Method of Control, 164

Organizational Effective-
ness, 21, 199, 204,
207, 208, 209
Organizational Effective-
ness, Factors Affecting,
211
Organizational Effi-
ciency, 199, 202
Organizational Health,
200
Organizational Problem
Solving, 20, 125
Organizational Problem
Solving Through Staff
Units, 193
Organizational Slack, 174

Paradigm, definition of,
7
Parsimony, definition of,
11
Plan (Planning), defini-
tion(s) of, 43, 78
Planning, Normative, 145
Plans as a Method of Co-
ordination, 171
Plausibility, definition
of, 12
Policy, definitions of,
43, 78
Power as a Method of
Control, 159
Precision, definition of,
10
Problem, definitions of,
75, 143
Problematic Situation,
definition of, 75
Problematic Situations,
Dimensions of, 77
Problems Attended to by
Coalitions, 69
Problem Solving, Norma-
tive, 144, 146

Problem Solving, Organiza-
tional, 125
Problem Solving, Problem
Formulation Phase of,
126, 128
Problem Solving, Problem
Recognition Phase of,
126, 128
Problem Solving, Search
Phase of, 126, 132
Procedural Sum of Pro-
cesses, definition of,
209
Process Active, definition
of, 6
Process Model, definition
of, 5
Process Passive, definition
of, 6
Processes, Procedural Sum
of, definition of, 209
Processes, Procedures for
Improving, 111, 199
Productivity (see Ef-
ficiency)
Programmed Procedures, 78

Reasoning as a Method of
Control, 154
Required Task Process
Changes, its Effects
upon Effectiveness, 214
Reward System (*See* Evalua-
tion System)
Rigidity, its Effects upon
Effectivenss, 89, 214
Rules as a Method of Con-
trol, 157

Schedules as a Method of
Coordination, 171
Search, Circumscribed, 134
Search, Depth of, 140
Search, Idiomatic, 138

Search, Locus of, 140
Search, Normative Pro-
    cedures for, 142
Search, Opportunistic, 137
Search, Problemistic, 134
Search, Reactive, 132
Side Payment, definition
    of, 39
Simplicity, definition of,
    11
Staff-Line (*See* Line-Staff)
Standard Operating Pro-
    cedure (SOP), 19, 74,
    77, 136, 195
SOPs, Designing and
    Altering, 82, 90, 195
SOPs, Their Effects Upon
    Organizational Be-
    havior, 87
SOPs as a Method of Con-
    trol, 157
State Description, defini-
    tion of, 3
State Transition Diagram,
    definition of, 4

Stimulus-Response (S-R)
    Paradigm, definition
    of, 8
S-R Goal Paradigm, 24
Strategy, definitions of,
    43, 78
Subunit Identification,
    32
System, definition of,
    2

Training as a Method of
    Control, 163
Training Groups (T-Groups),
    35

Uncertainty Avoidance,
    89, 136
Unprogrammed Procedures,
    78

Validity, definition of,
    10

Working to Rule, 158